# From the Cliffs of Pyla

# From the Cliffs of Pyla

*A Memoir*

## Karlan Strong

**To order additional copies of this book, contact:**
Xlibris Corporation
1-888-795-4274
www.Xlibris.com
Orders@Xlibris.com
80600

# *Acknowledgments*

My memoir has benefited from candid and insightful suggestions of family and friends. These include Gary and Paula Suttle and Barbara and Larry Mamlet. Members of The North County Writers Bloc of Carlsbad, California, listened to my chapters over and over again. They pushed and challenged me while endlessly encouraging my progress. Special thanks to our group leader Carol Saylor. *Karlen was in our writing class in Carlsbad.*

Beret Strong gave her highly professional editing skills with gracious goodwill. She asked intriguing questions that made me think beyond my memories and challenged me with comments such as, "How can the reader know you only spoke French?" and "The readers don't know the Joseph Smith story. Tell them." She gave me myriad, helpful nudges toward clarity and deeper revelations.

My heartfelt appreciation to Dr. Eduardo Val who, over many years, kept "righting the ship" when the going became too painful.

But it is to my husband, Doug, I owe all my thanks. His tireless, loving energy made it possible for me to gather up the threads of my life.

# A Path Chosen

If the past lies hidden
in words unspoken,
pain may fester
and shadows grow.

To find one's way
to freedom and light
is to risk the unknown
with no turning back.

Douglas Hillman Strong, 2010

# *Chapter One*

Paris—June, 1940

Bombs fell and everything shook. My sister, Joan, threw up. And no one got my breakfast. The trouble started when the baby got inside momma. The more she grew, the worse it got. My brother, Hal, he was twelve, said the baby had nothing to do with it.

"We're at war. That's what's going on. Germany is attacking France. Get it?"

I didn't 'get it'. "But we live in Paris," I said, twisting my hair around my finger.

"That's in France, goofy."

My sister, Joan, she was nine, didn't get it either. "But why did we come to Calais? The planes only dropped leaflets on us in Paris."

"Daddy had a meeting here," Hal said. "Remember? And he told us Calais was the best defended city in France."

When the sirens started again, we ran into the hall. A man yelled, "Go to the wine cellar. It's built like a fort."

I saw the elevator waiting for us. Hal pulled me away. "That's not safe. We have to go down the stairs."

My nurse, Mademoiselle Malmoray, cried in her handkerchief. She kept saying, "The Germans are coming, the Germans are coming."

The stone cellar had everyone crammed inside. Our waiter from the day before came over. I buried myself in nurse's long black skirt.

"A terrible thing. We'll do the same to Berlin. They'll be sorry."

Mademoiselle shook her head and moved away from him. Then I heard my daddy's voice.

"Are you all right?" He looked worried as he ducked into the cellar.

"Didn't you hear the sirens, the bombs?" Hal spoke first. "Where have you and mom been?"

"On the top floor terrace. We had been told by generals at the meeting last night to expect fireworks at five in the morning." Daddy spoke quietly but all the other people stopped talking to listen. "The military said we would see antiaircraft practice," he said. "They thought it would be a treat for your mother." Daddy came close to us. "No one expected an attack," he whispered. "I should have left all of you in Paris." He looked over at me, smiled, then picked me up. "Did the bombing scare you, Karlie?"

"Yes."

"You're a brave four-year-old." Daddy put me down with a pat on my head.

I stuck my thumb in my mouth to keep from crying. No one noticed.

"Where's mommy?" Joan sounded like she wanted to cry.

"Your mommy is resting. We had quite a morning."

"Is it safe to go upstairs?" the waiter asked.

"I think so." Daddy still looked worried.

"Monsieur Richard, tell me," the waiter went on, "do you know where they bombed?"

"Mostly the harbor, I've been told. It could have been worse."

Daddy went to my nurse. He didn't touch her but his voice sounded soft, like a hug.

"Mademoiselle Malmoray, would it please you if, after we pack our belongings in Paris, we go to our villa in Pyla?".

My nurse looked up at daddy. "Oh, Monsieur Richards, thank you. It has been a long time since our last visit. I hunger for my home at a time like this." My nurse's smile gave me goose bumps. She squeezed my hand tight. "We're going to Pyla-sur-mer at the Bay of Arcachon, little one. The sea will heal us."

# *Chapter Two*

"Can our momma bend?" I asked Joan.

"What do you mean, bend?"

"You know, daddy bends down to pick me up but our momma never bends."

"Oh, that's because she's a queen. Queens don't bend."

"Where's her crown?"

"Not that kind of a queen. If you're beautiful like our mommy, you're a queen and everybody—everyone looks at you. Anyway," Joan went on, "our mommy is pregnant so she can't bend."

That baby again.

Once I called my nurse, "momma." She looked over at Joan then whispered in my ear. "Don't call me that. I'm your nurse. You call the fancy lady momma but never me." She looked back at Joan. I guess to make sure she hadn't heard us. I was careful after that.

We all piled into daddy's new Buick and drove to Bordeaux. Joan and Hal were surprised when momma stayed at their friend's home. For once I knew something before they did. I had watched momma pack. She filled her suitcase with gowns. She never wore those clothes in Pyla. I knew we'd be at the villa without momma and daddy.

Daddy drove us to the sea but stayed only one night. He left before I got up. Joan cried because he hadn't said goodbye. I didn't care. I had my nurse.

The next night Mademoiselle wouldn't give me my special drink. Joan and Hal didn't know I had wine before I went to bed. I guess we didn't have enough for them.

"Why can't I have my drink tonight?" I felt like crying but only pouted.

"Not tonight, little one. Just go to sleep."

"I can't sleep without my wine." I went to bed but rolled over and over. Then the wind came from the sea. Wham, wham! The windows shook. "Mademoiselle, Mademoiselle," I whispered. No answer. She always slept right next to me but now she had gone. Maybe the wind came because of the war. Maybe planes made the wind. I got scared. Before I could cry out, she pulled me to her.

"Why are you dressed?" I asked. I couldn't stop the scared feeling.

"Don't make a sound," she spoke softly in my ear. "There's something I have to show you."

She pulled scratchy leggings on me, then Joan's old sweater that covered my hands. I tried to yank off the clothes. "It's night outside. I don't want to go out there. And I need to pee."

"Too much noise," she looked around the room. "I don't want Joan to hear. Joan can't keep a secret. And Hal . . . well."

Then she did a funny thing. She put my pillow and blanket in a sack. She pulled me out of the house and into the wind. I pulled back. I didn't like the dark or the wind or anything.

"It will blow me over," I cried.

"I'm here," she said.

When I looked at her, she had another big bag over her shoulder. How could she carry me?

"Walk in front of me, Karlie. I won't let you fall."

There was a little path right on the edge of the cliff. We were never allowed to go there because daddy said it was too dangerous. Way, way down the waves beat the rocks. But now we stood on that path in the dark with the wind trying to throw us off. I wet my leggings.

"Never mind, said Mademoiselle. "It doesn't matter."

I walked slow. I wanted to close my eyes and wake up later. I got down and crawled along the path. My nurse said something but I couldn't hear her. I got sick in my stomach. I tried to look at Mademoiselle but the wind hit my face. "Hug me, hug me, I'm sick." Maybe she couldn't hear me because she didn't pick me up.

"Keep going, little one." That's what she said over and over. I kept crawling.

"Stop," she said, "we're here."

The path became a wide patch of grass. I stood up. My nurse disappeared in the dark.

"Mademoiselle?" I called but only the wind said anything.

"It's here somewhere," I finally heard her say.

"What?" I asked. She didn't answer. I saw her then walking along the cliffs, feeling the rocks.

"Here it is!" For the first time she spoke loud. She pulled me to where some vines wrapped around a big rock. Then she disappeared again. I heard the match before I saw the light. The candle flickered. She stood in a cave, holding back the vines for me. No more wind. She put the bundles down and pulled me on her lap. She didn't care about my wet clothes.

"This was where I played as a child." She started rocking me. "Karlie, I'll never let the German's get you. If they should come and I'm not able . . .

if I can't get away, you run to this place. See, we have food, water, even blankets. You'll be safe. And I'll get to you as soon as I can."

Her face looked funny in the candlelight. I didn't like the cave. I wanted this bad dream to go away. But I kept the secret. We had so many together, Mademoiselle and me.

# Chapter Three

Finally daddy came in the Buick and took us back to Bordeaux.

"You're going to America," he said, "no more bombs, no more sirens."

Mademoiselle began to scream. "No, you can't take my Karlie. I'll keep her safe."

"Calm yourself," daddy said, "I'll return to Paris to pack. Everything will have to be shipped."

I didn't like the way my nurse's hands shook. It scared me. She took something out of a box with pretty paper and gave it to me. She never stopped crying and her nose kept running. She always wiped my nose. I didn't know what to do.

"I made this for you, my sweet child." I looked at the pretty blue coat with pearl buttons and almost felt better.

"I sewed it all by hand." My nurse made more big gulping sounds. She pushed the coat to me. I stroked it like I did our cook's kitten. My coat felt soft, softer even then little Duveux. I went dizzy maybe because I got only a few bites of my bread with chocolate on top. I wanted my secret wine. I wanted to go to sleep.

"This coat will protect you from everything," nurse tried to smile. "Think of me and pray to Jesus. Nothing bad can happen to you." Then she started crying again so hard her face looked ugly.

Momma came in. She looked cross. "Mademoiselle Malmoray, do not scream in front of the child. We are all having to do difficult things." She went to daddy. She started talking in English so I couldn't understand.

I pulled on Joan's hand. She knew a little English.

"Mommy doesn't want to go without daddy," she said. "And he said, 'France is falling.'"

Where was France falling? Maybe over the cliff at Pyla. And what was the matter with Hal. He just sat there in a blanket not talking when I asked him questions.

"He has pneumonia," daddy told me. He didn't explain the word like he usually did. No one explained anything and my nurse kept crying. Daddy said something about the *S.S Washington* and Le Verdun-sur-mer.

"What, what?" I asked Joan.

"I think it's a ship," she said. "It's stopping in Le Verdun-sur-mer just for us."

"Is daddy coming after he packs everything?"

"I don't think so."

"Why?"

Joan just shook her head like she always did when she couldn't understand all the English words. Then Hal said something so quietly I had to go right over to his chair to hear him.

"Daddy's a diplomat, that's why. He has to go to Germany and learn all he can. He said he has to go 'before it's too late.'" Then Hal leaned back and went to sleep.

# *Chapter Four*

I saw the ship first as we drove over the hill. When our Buick stopped, a strange man ran up to daddy. He looked dirty. I crawled back into the car. Something was wrong with the man. Daddy had to hold him up.

"I think mom and dad know him," Hal said. He hadn't spoken all during the ride. Now he whispered to me, "Look, Karlie, that's old blood on his uniform—And, and bullet holes!"

"Good Lord, Allen, what happened?" Momma stepped close to him.

"I heard the ship was stopping here for your family. My wife is on board. I slipped out of the hospital. Grabbed my uniform. I have to say goodbye to her. The Captain won't let me search. Karl, help me."

"When were you wounded?" asked my daddy.

"Dunkirk," he said. I wondered what day of the week that was.

Momma hurried to look for his wife. Too many people, she couldn't find her.

"Tell her how hard I tried," he said to momma. Then he walked away, crying.

The captain came up to daddy. "We must leave at once, Monsieur Richards."

He spoke in French and smiled at me. I liked him. The ship looked big and scary but at least those Germans couldn't get us. Daddy stayed on the shore by his Buick and waved. He got smaller and smaller until I couldn't see him anymore.

Momma stayed quiet a long time. Finally she said, "We're lucky to have a private stateroom. Everyone else is doubled up." But she sounded sad.

And I didn't feel lucky. My nurse got left. The cook didn't come, not even the kitten. I didn't know the tall, beautiful lady very good. But I called her, "momma."

It got worse. In the middle of the night, the door flew open. I bumped my head. The ship had stopped. There stood the Captain.

He sounded cross but I couldn't understand him. Hal told me we had to get on deck because . . . . But he didn't finish. Then momma spoke in French.

"We didn't hear an alarm. What's happened now?"

The Captain said something to our stewart. They spoke in English.

"Tell me what they're saying, Hal, please." I stared at my brother. His eyes got big. He looked whiter than ever. He must be getting sicker.

"Ten minutes," Hal said, finally. "We have just ten minutes to get in the lifeboats. Then—then the Germans will blow up the ship."

Those Germans again.

I wouldn't leave without my special coat. I tore everything apart until I found it. It had hidden between my sister's sweater and momma's hat.

"We can go now," I told everyone. "We just have to pray to Jesus and I wear the magic coat."

It was cold and black on deck. People hurried everywhere. Little boats on the side hung over the ocean by ropes. They were full of mommas and kids. I did my praying and sucked my thumb. No one scolded me. I got pushed along until I looked into the face of a lady in one of the little boats. She reached out her arms. I started to fall to her when momma pulled me back.

"No, I won't risk it," she held my arm tight. "Hal is too sick and I'm too pregnant."

That baby again.

The lifeboats slipped down, down into the water but the ropes held them close to the ship. Everything went quiet. We stood with the daddies left on board. Why didn't momma look scared? She didn't scream or cry. She wasn't like my nurse. Maybe queens don't get frightened. The wind blew but not as hard as when we were on the path in Pyla. The black sky felt the same, though. Hal pulled me into his blanket. He shivered but felt hot.

I didn't expect the ship to move. But it did, slowly at first then faster, faster. The people in the little boats had a bumpy time. After awhile, the sailors pulled up the lifeboats and everyone got out. When the sky got lighter, the submarine could see our name, S. S. *Washington,* so they didn't blow us up. At least that was what my brother said.

Hal told me we got in trouble when we went some place without permission from the Germans. But we didn't stop being bad. We sneaked all over the place picking people up in Lisbon and Ireland. The new passengers had to sleep on the deck. All the time, we stayed scared about the German submarines. At least Hal got better and answered all my questions again.

The captain said momma had to live in the ship hospital so she wouldn't lose the baby. Joan cut out a strip of paper every morning to keep track of how long we crisscrossed the ocean trying to keep away from U-boats. That's what Hal called them. Sixteen strips of paper were stuck on the bulletin board before we saw momma again. She didn't lose the baby.

Hal told me even the Italians got mad at France and England. He said they had U-boats, too. Maybe they were mad at me. I twisted my hair around my finger and pulled.

I didn't know what country I came from. I belonged to Mademoiselle Malmoray. I must be French.

# *Chapter Five*

When we landed in America, lots of ships honked at us. They sounded like cows. Paper ribbons came flying from the sky. People I didn't know hugged me. Momma tried to pull off my blue coat. I held on tight. I didn't care about hot sun.

One woman patted my head over and over. She called me, "*ma petit refugiee.*"

"What does that mean, Joannie?"

"It means we have no home."

That made me sad. I stuck my thumb in my mouth. Joan must have been right because we kept getting on trains, staying in strange houses then getting on trains again. Everywhere we went people said daddy was a hero because he saved their friends from the Germans. "A brave man," they called him. Hal told me about it because now I couldn't understand anything.

Momma said I had to learn English so Joan and Hal should stop speaking French. They whispered French in my ear, anyway. I wouldn't listen to English. I didn't like the noise it made. I could hear birds sing in French but English sounded like sharp stones. It made me think about the rocky path in Pyla.

In one house we stayed longer than usual. I sat by myself in a big room, my blue coat bunched up on my lap. Everyone else had gone into the basement for a party. Nobody cared if I stayed alone as long as I didn't touch anything.

A big picture hung over the fireplace. It had angry paint everywhere. The colors didn't like each other. They fought but didn't move. I hated the painting. The sound of English felt the same, full of ugly. I made my eyes stay on the picture. I twirled my hair around my finger. I stared until the colors rolled together. Finally, they spilled out of the painting onto the floor. Then the colors disappeared. It made me smile. I liked that I could do that. Mademoiselle Malmoray said I had nightmares in the day. She said my head made them. Those nightmares scared me but making colors go away felt good. If only I could make English disappear.

Momma got telegrams from the government telling her about daddy. One telegram said that someone called "Gestapo" had daddy and wouldn't let him go. Momma sat still when she got that telegram. She looked out the window all afternoon but didn't talk.

Then one day daddy called on the phone. Momma said the call came from London. Now she looked different. She sat in front of the mirror and brushed her hair. Tears ran over her face. She said daddy had adventures and would tell us all about them.

Finally, I understood why daddy took so long. He had to find my nurse in the cave. Daddy would come in the door and right behind him would be Mademoiselle Malmoray. I almost couldn't breath, I felt so happy.

Daddy walked into the house alone. Everyone jumped up and down. They all talked at once. I went to bed even though the sun still sat in the sky. I made a pillow of my blue coat. I didn't listen to daddy's stories. Besides he told them in English. My birthday, that was when my nurse would come—for sure, on my birthday.

# *Chapter Six*

We got on the train again and went for a long time to where it always rained. I wanted to get back on the train but momma said she loved green so we stayed put in Seattle. No one asked me where I wanted to live.

One day we went to a big party given just for us, well for daddy, the hero. But he was late again. Everyone waited and waited for him. It fussed momma when he came late. I stood on the porch by a table full of food. I stuck my finger into the dripping frosting on the cake. Sun had finally come to Seattle. Momma grabbed my arm. She must be cross with my licking the frosting but she hadn't noticed.

"We're taking a walk. Hurry."

Oh, good, she spoke to me in French.

"The woman who owned a house near here died recently," she told me.

I quickly made the sign of the cross.

"Karlan, don't do that. We're not Catholics, for goodness sake. That's all behind you. We're Mormons. Forget everything Mademoiselle Malmoray told you."

"What's a Mormon, momma?"

She didn't answer.

"We need a place to live," she told me while pulling me along. "We can't afford to buy a house. We'll have to rent. We don't have a spoon of our own, not a tea cup. But if we could find something here, right here in Hunts Point, I—I wouldn't feel so punished."

Momma seemed to be talking to herself even if she did it in French.

"Maybe we can rent this house," she went on. "I have to have a home to bring my baby. He's coming soon." It was the first time I heard momma sound scared. "We've lost everything . . . everything to the war." Momma looked around like she wanted someone to jump out of the bushes and help her. I didn't know what to do. I twisted my hair around my finger. We found the driveway but could see only trees. We walked along until we came to a brick path. Still no house. I wanted to play in the pond we found that had water coming over a stone wall. I saw goldfish and two frogs but momma wouldn't let me stay.

Finally we got to the house. On the porch sat three angry old ladies. Maybe they were witches. They each sat on rocking chairs going back and forth, back and forth. They didn't look happy to see us. Momma stopped speaking French so I didn't know what she said. But all three shook their heads, "no." Momma made an awful sound, like an animal in a trap.

"What's wrong, what happened?" I pulled on her arm.

"They won't rent the house to us." Momma started to turn around.

Then, one of the ladies stood up. She came right over to me, like she had been waiting for me. She had white hair cut short. The skin on her face looked like crushed up tissue paper. Her purple dress shimmered. "Hello, little one." She spoke French. It was the first time anyone, except my family, and the lady on the dock, knew how to talk to me. She took my hand. Her face looked happy, all the anger gone. Maybe it's what speaking French does for people.

She took me into the house and down a long hall to a room with a piano that played all by itself. I sat on the bench and pretended I did the playing. I could see myself in the shiny wood floors. I didn't know what to look at next. A picture of a swan made me stop. Oh, and over there, a big elephant.

"It's made of porcelain," said the lady. "I have more. Call me Aunt Mildred. Now come along, child."

She took me to another room with lots of soft chairs and a magic box you put to your eyes and look at pictures that turn real. I didn't want to put it down but she said, "Come." She seemed so excited, I couldn't help but skip behind her. She brought me into a big bright space with a giant piano that she called a "Steinway." On top sat a glass bowl of candy. She told me to take all I wanted and put more in my pocket for later on.

"Do you have a spoon or teacup?" I asked.

Aunt Mildred looked surprised. She took my hand again and brought me to a room off the kitchen. All the walls had shelves with glass doors and pretty handles. Inside I could see white dishes with flowers around the edges. In the drawers were lots of knives, forks and spoons.

Next she took me to the best place of all, a deep back porch with a roof on it. It went from one end of the house to the other. I sat with her on a swinging couch and looked down the long grassy hill.

"See all that blue water?" Aunt Mildred looked right at me. "That's Lake Washington. The little boat house at the bottom of the hill has a sailing dinghy inside." We rocked back and forth.

"My sister's name was Winona," Aunt Mildred told me. "She and her husband traveled all over the world. That's why there are so many interesting things in the house. But now . . . ." She stopped talking and just rocked. I watched her face. Finally she started talking again. But just like with momma she forgot I was there.

"I've been here with my two sisters for ten days—about nine days too long." She said that last part in an angry voice. "We can't decide what to do. Should we divide everything between us? Should we give it all away? What would Winona want? That's what I care about." I saw tears in the corner of her eye. "It's a terrible thing when sisters can't get along."

Aunt Mildred looked sad. I didn't like that so I took her hand.

She sighed, smiled at me. Now I felt better.

"Aunt Mildred, do you know what a Mormon is?"

"Good heavens, child, what made you ask that? It's some kind of religion. I don't know much more than that." She gave another long sigh. "I think I know what Winona would want us to do. We can't rent because, mercy knows, we sisters don't want to ever come back here. But we can sell this place to you and your family with everything inside. We can do that much for Winona."

# *Chapter Seven*

Morgan got born. He and momma stayed a long time in the hospital. We moved into the magic house without them.

"Mother almost died," Joan whispered. "Infection."

She tucked me into bed. I made the sign of the cross, dreamed of Mademoiselle. I woke up screaming.

"Just a nightmare," Joan hugged me.

The bed was all wet. Joan put me in clean pajamas. But I couldn't stop crying.

"Joannie, I hurt again in—that place."

"Shhh," said Joan. "It will go away." She took me into her bed. "Mademoiselle said to press on the spot when it hurts," Joan said. "Try rocking. That might help."

"What's going to happen, Joannie? Can we go back to Paris now?"

"No, no, the war's there. Remember, Karlie, Mademoiselle always called you her little witch? That's because you're strong and—and I guess she meant magical. So now you have to be a strong little witch."

I felt better in Joan's bed. She spoke French to me when we were alone. I didn't want to but I began to understand English. I never spoke it, though.

Finally momma and the baby came home. Daddy brought me to meet my brother. I didn't see Morgan at first. My eyes went to the big bed. The woman in it looked white like the sheets. Her eyes weren't momma's blue eyes. They were like rain water in a puddle. Daddy brought me to the corner of the room, near the big windows. A black-haired woman with a long chin sat in a rocking chair. Her dress was ugly brown. She held a baby.

"This little fellow is your brother," said my daddy, like he was giving me a present or something. "And this is Sister Root who will be helping mommy take care of Morgan."

I backed away fast. I barely looked at my brother. Sister Root smelled bad. Her dark eyes went over me like a snake ready to bite. I made the hex sign, tore down to the boat house. When I opened the door, Sister Root came out of the shadows twice as big. I knew she wasn't real but I screamed anyway. She was a day-nightmare. I couldn't run back to the house. The real Sister Root was there. I couldn't go to the boat house. The bad-dream Sister Root lived there. I sat on the grass and twisted my hair.

Daddy went away again. Sister Root stayed. She made icky food, ground up stuff with thick, black sauce. She tried to make me take cod liver oil. Joan hugged me a lot. Hal rode his bike all the way across the bridge and got a job. He washed dishes. He brought home good stuff to eat.

Momma got up at night. She walked outside in her nightgown. I watched from my window. She looked like a ghost.

One morning, Sister Root wasn't in the kitchen. Momma stood in her place trying to make oatmeal.

"Where's Sister Root?" Joan asked.

Momma didn't answer.

The next day, Joan and Hal went to school. Joan wore the red sweater Grandfather Lafount sent her.

Momma said, "Don't wear that good sweater."

"I want to look nice—so, so kids will like me," Joan held tight to the sweater.

Momma didn't say, "no."

In the afternoon clouds came. Momma got more and more upset. She walked from window to window saying, "The rain is coming. Everything is ruined, ruined."

She didn't notice me. She didn't see Morgan either. He cried in a hiccuping way. Joan had fed him before she left. But momma didn't feed him. I tried to give him water in a glass. It made him all wet and he choked. I covered him up with blankets. Hurry up Joan. Get home quick. I was getting upset like momma.

Then the rain broke through the sky. It fell like a river. I could see Joan stumbling. She had the red sweater under her shirt. That was smart, Joan, good for you. Momma ran out in the rain with a broom. She screamed things but I only understood the word "ruined." She hit Joan with the broom handle. I tried to grab the broom. Momma didn't notice. Then Hal came home. I don't know what happened next. Sister Root came back, momma disappeared.

When daddy got home, Joan ran to him. "Our mother has turned into a bad witch. She has to go away forever."

I waited by the door to find out if we could get rid of momma.

But daddy said, "What a wicked thing to say. You have a wonderful mother. She's ill, very ill. Not her fault."

Daddy took me away to a little chicken farm far in the country. Right away I liked Mutti Mega. She didn't speak English and she couldn't speak French. I didn't know what she said. I didn't miss words. Mutti Mega was all over round and doughy. She had little teeth like Joan. She didn't have much hair. What she had was soft, like clouds, a little puff here, another one there.

I climbed a ladder to a spot under the eaves. I slept on a feather bed. I had another feather quilt on top. I wondered if her hair was in my soft bed. Maybe that was why she didn't have much.

We gathered eggs together. We gardened. We made bread and pies. She rocked me on her lap. Mutti Mega sang all the time. She could even whistle. I tried, but couldn't get it. My trying made her laugh. We stayed happy together for so many days I forgot about momma and Sister Root. Sometimes I thought about Joan and Hal. Then I felt sad but Mutti Mega noticed and sang me a song.

When daddy came to pick me up, I begged to stay. I didn't ever want to go back to that house. Mutti Mega and I cried and cried.

On the way home, daddy told me my birthday had come and gone.

"Did Mademoiselle Malmoray come looking for me?"

Daddy turned to me. "No, Karlie." He patted my leg. "She is still in France. Probably in Pyla. She won't ever be coming here."

I didn't care about missing my birthday. I looked out the window but didn't see anything.

Morgan was big and crawling when I got home. He made a lot of noise. He pulled himself up in the crib and rocked it hard. He climbed over the bars and landed with a thump. He didn't cry. I didn't play with him. I stayed by myself. I saw him sit on the top step of the stairs and let himself bounce down to the bottom. As soon as he could walk, he got all the way down to the lake. A neighbor called on the phone.

"Your naked baby's at the end of the dock. He's ready to jump in. Hurry."

Joan always hurried after Morgan. Sister Root had gone. Joan, she was ten. She did most of the work. Joan didn't have time for me. Hal went to his job after school and on weekends.

I heard my momma laughing one morning. At first I didn't know who it could be. I found her giving Morgan a bath. She called him "beautiful baby." I didn't go in. I just watched and let myself feel good.

Then Morgan came down with the measles. Daddy had already left for a long trip. He thought everything was fine. He had played lots with me and Morgan. He made Hal, Joan and me ice cream sodas. He built a huge playpen down by the lake so Morgan could dig in the sand or play in the grass.

After Morgan got sick, momma began talking to the windows again and walking outside in the dark. She didn't take care of Morgan, just like before. He felt hot like a stove. When Joan left for school, I tried to keep a cold cloth on his head. I saw Joan doing that. I tried talking to momma. I even tried to talk to her in English but she didn't notice.

"Baby sick," I pulled on her arm.

Momma went outside and started walking. I didn't want to leave Morgan. Finally Joan came home.

"Joannie, don't go to school anymore."

The next morning momma told Joan she had to go to school and so did Hal. Momma didn't pay any attention to Morgan. She wouldn't listen to me. Morgan stopped crying after awhile. I tried to give him a bottle but he wouldn't drink. The milk ran all over his face. Just when Hal and Joan got home from school, Morgan stopped moving but his eyes stayed open. Hal ran to the neighbors. The police came. Momma didn't notice.

After Morgan left the hospital, he went with daddy on the train to Detroit, Michigan. Morgan lived with Aunt Lenore and Uncle George for a long, long time. Aunt Lenore was momma's sister.

Momma came back from the hospital after Morgan left. She sat and looked out the window but she didn't scream anymore or walk outside in her nightgown.

# *Chapter Eight*

I didn't want to be in the magic house. I found a soft patch of grass in the woods next to us. I sat with my knees pulled to my chest and rocked. I moaned in a soft singing way that made me feel peaceful.

"Why are you doing that?" said a voice.

I looked up to the bluest eyes I had ever seen. She was my age and standing half behind a tree. Her full lips looked chapped and red, her wavy hair held sunlight.

"I hurt," I said. "Do you . . . hurt?"

"No! Why do you talk funny."

"I speak French. English, not so good." I waited to see if she'd run away. I wanted her to stay. "You see things?" I tried to think of the right English word. "Things not real?"

"No."

"I mean, awake, like dream—in day."

"No." She stepped back, behind the tree.

"Do you see," I spread my arms wide and made a circle, "light around . . . people, trees?"

"Yes!" she shouted and came right up to me. "What color do you see around me?"

She looked excited.

"White-yellow, a little blue," I told her.

"I see you mostly orange and, and kind of green blue, not much white. I guess it's because you hurt."

After that day, I forgot all about my brother Morgan and I didn't think too much about momma or what had happened to her. I had a best friend, Sharon Sleigh. She lived right next door with just the skinny woods between us. Best of all, she saw lights like me.

I started speaking English all the time. First I only spoke with Sharon, then I forgot to go back to French when I went home.

Sharon and I built forts and told each other secrets. We got naked together, rolled in the mud, then we'd dance. Finally, we washed off in the lake. No one ever found out.

Sharon's mommy and daddy left her home alone at night. They went off square dancing and to movies. They locked the house up tight and took the key. They had a big pot belly stove to heat the house. It scared Sharon.

"What about a fire," she sobbed. I won't be able to get out." Sharon's eyes darted around the room as if she could see the fire that very minute. "I'll burn up."

"Nonsense," said her daddy. "There won't be a fire if you don't open the front of the stove."

I listened along with Sharon but I felt afraid too. I thought of bombs, fires, people screaming. I didn't want her left alone.

We could hear Sharon crying when her parents drove away. I couldn't stand it. I wanted to go to her but I felt afraid of the woods at night. I begged Hal or Joan to go with me. One of them always did. We'd talk to Sharon through the screen to make her feel better.

One night, Hal had an idea.

"Come on," he said to me. He put his feet into father's big muddy boots that stood handy at the door. Galumph, galumph, galumph, he plodded

through the mud to Sharon's house. Hal went to the open window that had
a heavy screen nailed tight. He cut the corner of the screen with his sharp
Swiss Army knife.

"See Sharon," said Hal. "You can pull out the screen if you have to and
jump through the window. I mean, if a fire should come."

The plan worked super great. Sharon's father found the cut screen and
saw the footprints. They looked big. I guess Sharon's father got scared,
not about a fire, but about a stranger in the woods. Sharon's grandmother
moved into the little house and everyone was happy—especially Sharon.

Sharon did make-believe even better than me. The whole afternoon
we would do one long adventure tale. She'd start and I'd butt in then she'd
butt back in, "No, no the worm knew about the treasure but couldn't see so
couldn't tell so he was safe for the dragon to trust." And then I'd say, "But
the princess gave the worm eyes to see and the worm got more powerful
than the dragon." We never got tired of each other.

# Chapter Nine

I started first grade with Sharon. I liked recess and riding the school bus. I didn't like much else.

The principal called momma.

"Come to my office after school and bring Karlan."

The principal had thick eyebrows. They sat bunched up over her nose when she talked. She had a waxy face. I thought if she smiled it might break into little pieces.

"I'm sorry, Mrs. Richards," she said, "but we aren't able to handle a child like Karlan. She's unteachable." The principal didn't look at me, only my momma. "It isn't just that she doesn't know her letters or numbers. Even when we work with her, she twitches and talks to herself."

I sat still like a stone. I didn't even touch my hair. Then she stared right at me. Her mouth looked like she enjoyed eating spiders.

"She doesn't know a single nursery rhyme."

"She knows them in French." Momma only whispered this. I pushed her hand so she would say it louder.

The principal didn't pay any attention. She looked down at her desk. "And," she said in a mean voice, "she keeps touching herself in—well—in the private place." She whispered that part like someone outside the window might hear her. "We can't have that in our school."

Momma didn't say anything. She took my hand and we left. I felt sick to my stomach. Would momma start talking to windows again? She looked so sad and daddy had gone on one of his trips.

When we got home, she made tea for both of us. She read my tea leaves and told me they said not to worry. I had a good brain. She said the leaves told her I would stop hurting soon in the private place.

I felt brave. "Momma, that bad lady has icky light around her. That's why she's so mean."

Momma went frozen. "What are you talking about?"

"Auras, momma. Mademoiselle said I see auras. That's how I know what people are like inside."

"Auras! No! Only people who are . . . ." Momma got up and walked around the kitchen. Maybe she was looking for something. Finally, she came back and sat in front of me. Her voice sounded sad. "Mademoiselle Malmoray put a—a wicked thought into your mind."

I wished I hadn't said anything about auras. Now mommy looked all upset again. She took a deep breath and reached for my hand.

"But it's important, Karlan, that you don't touch yourself. That makes people, well, uncomfortable. They don't want you around."

Momma's eyes still looked sad but she smiled at me. "If you stop seeing strange things, people will like you."

I tried to smile at momma. I didn't want her mad at me.

"Now that you will be home, Karlan, I can teach you nursery rhymes in English." Momma got up and cleared away our tea cups.

"You and I can shell the peas for dinner. You can be my helper when Joan's away at school."

I nodded my head and tried to look happy but I had a lump in my stomach. I had to be careful what I told my momma.

# *Chapter Ten*

I didn't go back to school until the next year so I started first grade all over again. That was okay except Sharon had moved up to the second grade. During the year I stayed home, I learned lots of nursery rhymes and how to spell my name. My English got pretty good. I forgot all my French. I didn't even feel scared when I started school again. I'd probably be the smartest kid in my class. I sure was the biggest.

Daddy told me he had trouble with reading, too. And he said he had to use a typewriter because no one could read his writing.

"I'm still a poor speller." He didn't sound ashamed about it. "Someday you'll have a secretary like I do. Then no one will know anything about your problem because she'll keep quiet."

We sat together in the sun room with the piano that played by itself. It seemed special to be alone with daddy. I felt important.

"Why do you go away so much?" I looked right at him.

He didn't answer for a long time. I saw his eyes turn into lakes.

"Shouldn't have gone after Morgan's birth. Should have stayed home with your mother." He didn't seem to be talking to me.

"But why did you go?" I wouldn't give up.

He finally looked at me. "Because I thought—ahh, I thought it—vital." Father stood up, walked to the big windows. "I took trips to explain how

strong Germany had become. I wanted America to get ready for war." He
sat down again and took my hand. "I knew the war had to come. I didn't
want this country to fall like France. Remember the bombs? I didn't want
that happening here."

I felt cold all over. I remembered the bombs. But my dreams kept being
about Mademoiselle screaming, "The Germans are coming." I felt good
that my daddy had stopped those Germans from bombing our house in
Hunts Point.

Daddy stopped talking. He just sat. I wanted him to keep telling me
stuff so I pulled his hand. Finally, he looked at me again.

"Some people, important people, said we shouldn't go to war. Others
said it would be over in a few months. I knew better and . . . ."

I stopped him. "Sharon said Pearl Harbor means we're fighting with
Japan. Is Japan near Germany?"

Daddy got out a big map and showed me the countries fighting us. I
asked him lots of questions. I couldn't stop my mouth. I felt better about
things. I decided I had a smart daddy so I didn't have to worry if I ended
up like him. I felt good inside all day but when I fell asleep, I heard screams
and dreamed bombs were falling on our house and Sharon couldn't get out
her locked door.

Daddy took me on a trip to the country. He wouldn't tell me where. I
hoped I would see Mutti Mega again. But he took me to a farm with two
little girls my age. Daddy said they were a Japanese family. We bought
lots of painted birds the Japanese daddy had cut from wood. The family
seemed sad. On the way home, daddy told me that bad things were
happening to the Japanese in our country. He said he and other people
would try to save their farms. I liked him helping the little girls. I liked
having a hero for a daddy.

Just when things got comfortable, daddy told me, "Now we're moving to a brand new state. We're going to Michigan."

He showed me on the map. I pushed the map away. I wanted nothing to do with Michigan. Daddy didn't care. He paid no attention when I tried to tear up the map. "I'm not going to work for the government anymore," he said. "Maybe I won't travel so much." He kept smiling but I didn't smile back.

"I'm going to work for Uncle George," he told me. "Now we'll all be together with Morgan again."

I didn't want to leave. No one cared. I felt dizzy. I saw Lake Washington getting huge, like a wave about to swallow me up. I knew the wave couldn't be real but I saw it anyway. I told Sharon. She hugged me. We promised to find each other when we became grownups.

# *Chapter Eleven*

I hated Grosse Pointe, Michigan. The day we moved in, a golf ball came right through our front window.

"See, it's a sign we shouldn't be here," I said. I had a scared feeling all over and ran for the blue coat. I dumped everything out of my suitcase but the coat had disappeared.

"Oh, that old thing," said momma, "I threw it out."

I walked across the golf course to get to school. I lay down in each sand trap and made angels. Sometimes I could get three in one trap.

"Why are you covered in sand?" demanded my grumpy teacher. I gave her "the shrug."

Kids called me "retard", "Bugs Bunny" and "gopher guts." I hit them, threw stuff, yelled. I got into trouble, not them. Lots of times, I sneaked out of school. No one said anything. I wandered around thinking about the one good thing in the whole state of Michigan—my cousin Lynn. She didn't call me names. Lynn lived in Detroit so I only saw her at church on Sundays.

I had to pay attention when I went off on my own because I got mixed up and lost. Once a policeman helped me when I couldn't find my street.

"Why aren't you in school?" He looked suspicious.

"I fell off the slide and hurt my head," I lied. "The teacher sent me home." I let my head tilt to the side and gave a soft moan.

That night I sat at the dining room table mushing my food, not eating. Daddy looked at me. He started to say, "Don't play . . . ." but then he stopped.

"Good news, Karlan," he said instead.

I waited, not hoping for much.

"You're going to get braces."

"That's good news?" I sank deep into my chair.

"But that's great news," my fifteen-year-old brother, Hal, said. "Now the kids won't call you 'Bugs Bunny.'"

"And," my father went on, "you get to ride the bus all the way to the Henry Ford Hospital. And, you and my secretary, Miss Painter, can have lunch together."

"The bus? I ride the bus—alone? I'll get lost. I always get lost. You'll never see me again." I started crying. "I'm only eight-years-old."

Now I felt desperate. My hands got sticky wet. My stomach turned inside out. School felt safer. I didn't know where to hide or what to do.

Hal found me on the icy porch.

"You trust me when I'm teaching you to ice-skate, right?" he said

He sat one step above me. I could hear his teeth chattering.

"And you trusted me when I taught you to ride a bike, right?"

I nodded my head.

"Trust me now." He put his hands on my cold arms. "Bus drivers take care of kids like you. They'll tell you when to get off, the next bus to take, plus it will all be written down. Once you know how to get around on buses, you'll be freeee—as a bird."

He said the last part slow like a wizard's promise. I looked up at him.

"Come inside, goofy," he said. "I'm freezing."

That night I didn't have a nightmare. For the first time, I dreamed I could fly. I left the earth, went into the blackness of space. I woke up with something new inside me.

The just-for-people-underground-tunnel turned out way better than my sister Joan said. It connected all the downtown buildings. After I saw the dentist, I took the elevator to the basement of the hospital. I started walking. Big signs said which tunnel to take for which building. I stopped and pulled out the paper telling me where to go. My father worked in The New Center Building. I couldn't read but I could see the matching letters.

I didn't feel scared, not after how nice the bus drivers had been. The first one let me sit right behind him. He told me all the streets we passed and stuff about different neighborhoods. He gave me the number of the transfer bus. The next driver told me about braces and how good I'd feel when my teeth didn't stick out.

I stopped in the tunnel to listen. I liked the echo of secretaries rushing along on their spiked heels. I looked at the little shops. I ran my hand along the smooth wall with the cold butterscotch tiles. I'd tell Lynn all about it.

I got on the elevator in The New Center Building. Two secretaries were talking about Miss Painter. I looked straight ahead. My ears got every whispered word.

"She's sweet," said one. "She'll help you. You can ask her anything."

"It is so true," answered the other. "But what a shame, she's as plain as an old turnip."

Poor Miss Painter.

When I opened the door of my father's office, I saw a warm light, then a person in the middle with a long face, small green eyes and a big smile.

"I'm looking for Miss Painter."

"That's me," she beamed. When she stood up, my eyes got big. She kept unfolding out of the chair until she became as tall as my father.

"Karlan, at last." She hugged me. "We'll have so much fun together."

I could tell by her eyes we would.

"How about a chocolate milk shake and a hamburger? I'm starved," she said.

I studied her face all through lunch. She had teeth that stuck out like mine. Right on the tip of her long nose she had a crease. It looked like two noses were thinking about being born at once. I wanted to rub my finger in that little ridge but I didn't. She had a small deep scar on her cheek that kept moving when she talked. I imagined a dimple that had gotten confused and lost. I loved Miss Painter's face. She smelled wonderful too—like typewriter ribbon. I felt safe. I couldn't stop talking. I told her all about Lynn.

"What does she look like?" she asked.

"She's sooo pretty. She has these thick dark braids," I said. "It isn't fair. I'm stuck with baby hair that won't ever grow up."

"But your hair's soft, like spun gold."

I touched my hair, liking it better already.

"Lynn doesn't see lights around people like I do." I wadded up my napkin and put it in my full water glass. "It's okay, though. She doesn't call me names."

"Who calls you names?" Miss Painter looked angry.

Her upset made me warm all over. I told her about school. She kept shaking her head.

"Miss Painter, you have lots of happy light around you."

"Oh, good," she answered.

When Daddy said we were moving again, this time to Detroit, I jumped up and down. Detroit had wonderful people like Lynn, Miss Painter and bus drivers. We'd leave the miserable school behind.

# Chapter Twelve

"Did you know Joseph Smith had visions? He believed they came from God. Poor Joseph Smith." I sat on the edge of the back seat of our car leaning as close as I could to my parents in front. Both sat stiff. Neither turned to look at me. Joan, sitting next to me, pushed me in the ribs.

"Shhh. They did come from God."

"But I have them, too," I said. "I see things no one else sees. Not all the time but once in awhile. I know they're not real. Joseph Smith didn't understand that his mind made those things up."

When we got home mother talked to me.

"Don't ever tell anyone you see things that aren't real. Your mind is growing up like your body. But in the meantime, don't talk about auras or visions with anyone."

Mother looked unhappy, almost frightened. "You didn't tell Lynn, did you?"

I hadn't but I wondered why she'd worry about my "visions" when everyone at church felt happy about Joseph Smith.

The worst part of Sunday school came when everyone my age sat in a circle taking turns reading *The Book of Mormon*. We were in a corner of the basement recreation room. It was warm and happy for parties and dances.

Now it felt cold, ugly. Ten of us sat on fold-up chairs. No one looked scared but I was. I could never read those big words. How could I disappear? Maybe I could say I had to go to the bathroom then hide until church let out. The book landed on my lap. My hands got wet. I looked at it for a long time. I felt that funny flutter feeling in my chest. Sometimes it came when I got excited. Now it came when I felt stupid. The words swam all over the page. I took a deep breath and tried, "And—it—had—co . . . ."

Kids started to giggle. I glanced at Lynn. She bit her lip. She looked miserable like I felt. Everyone started laughing. I kept my head down. My face burned. A boy gently took the book out of my hands. I looked up into his grey-blue eyes. I almost cried for the kindness in them.

"I'm Bob Andrew," he said. "My twin brother, Chad, is over there. Don't worry about reading. We'll do it for you."

Everyone took a turn speaking in the big chapel, even kindergarten kids. I didn't mind standing up and telling grownups a story. I liked to give "two-and-a-half-minute-talks." Mostly no one helped me. I thought of a tale with a moral and wove it into a speech. I made my stories exciting, using different voices. I liked the looks I got and people coming up to me afterwards saying I did a good job.

Once I told about a boy who threw rocks into a pond, causing waves that destroyed his younger brother's sand castle.

"Mean words do that," I told the church people. "The pain goes on and on."

I made up the story to give a message to my mother. I wanted her to stop saying mean things to Joan. A few days earlier I found my sister crying in our room.

"Mother said I look lumpy." Joan's hugged herself, her face blotched red. "I wish someone would invent a machine that could make me over. I don't want to look like me anymore."

I didn't know what to tell her. I felt sad for Joan but steamy angry with our mother so I made up the story.

After church mother talked to me firmly, her face full of righteousness.

"I hope you'll take to heart," she said to me, "the message from your two-and-a-half-minute-talk. When you are rude to me, you hurt me very much."

"The story was about you," I yelled. "You're the one who says mean things. You called Joan 'lumpy' and made her cry."

"I don't remember saying that." Mother looked confused.

Maybe once the words came out, she forgot all about them.

I didn't use stories to tell mother anything after that. I yelled at her like I had yelled at the kids in Grosse Pointe. Sometimes I could see she looked afraid of me. I liked that fine.


Parts of church felt good, like the little speeches, spending time with Bob Andrew, and going to Lynn's house, but that didn't make me believe the Joseph Smith story.

I tried to imagine a fourteen-year-old boy kneeling in a grove praying. He said the sky suddenly opened up. An angel came surrounded by white light and told him to start a new church. I could believe that Joseph Smith saw lights around people but not the part about an angel from God. I felt powerful when I made the ugly painting disappear but I knew my mind did it. No one else saw what I saw. Joseph Smith, I figured, wanted to believe it all came from God so he had to convince everyone. He had to become a Prophet.

When I found my father alone, I told him. "I don't believe it."

"I questioned too." Daddy looked serious not angry. "But I've come to understand and so will you." He smiled and patted my hand. "Once you're baptized, your heart will open."

My daddy was my hero. I wanted to make him happy. Maybe magic happened. I just needed to believe and not think about it. I wanted to be like the rest of the family. I got baptized. I waited. And waited.

# *Chapter Thirteen*

I was playing roller derby with Miss Painter's chair. I pushed off one wall then slammed into another. I'd just made it all the way across the room when a tall lady came through the door. Her eyes grabbed me. I was so startled, my elbow hit the stapler. It crashed at her feet.

"I—I'm sorry." I jumped up from the chair, then stepped backwards toward Miss Painter.

"Trying to staple me to the floor or cripple me, huh—just to get out of my class?"

"No. I . . . your class?"

"I'm Miss Faucet. I am going to be your fifth grade teacher. Did you not know that?"

"No, Ma'am."

"Then I guess you don't know Miss Painter is my best friend. We meet for lunch every Saturday."

"No, Ma'am, I didn't know that either."

I didn't usually say, "ma'am" but something about Miss Faucet made me want to. Those gray eyes of hers could see right into my brain, I just knew it. I needed to say something, something good about myself.

"Bet I'll be the tallest kid in your class."

"Hmmmm, I think Benjamin Kline is about an inch taller. Do you know Benjie?"

"Sure, everyone knows him. He went to the regionals last year for the spelling bee. We're not friends or anything but he smiles at me sometimes."

"Do you like school, Karlan?"

"No, Ma'am, and it doesn't like me."

Miss Faucet stopped. She sat down as if she didn't want to eat lunch with Miss Painter after all. Her eyes changed again. Now I saw dark pools, but no sparkle.

"How did the school tell you it didn't like you?"

"Well, the building never said anything but teachers say I drive them crazy so I guess I mean the people in the school don't like me any more than I like them."

"That's about to change, Karlan. Ah, it looks like Miss Painter's ready for our lunch date. See you soon."


I stood in line with a bunch of other kids in front of Miss Faucet's classroom. We waited to begin our first day. The kids whispered about being scared.

"She's strict," said one kid who had lots of curly hair.

"Better not get on her bad side," whispered another.

When the bell rang, the door clicked open. Miss Faucet walked to her desk. She stood stone still, not looking at any of us. We took seats quickly. No one made a sound.

Finally she spoke, her voice deep and sad.

"The love of my life, Clark Gable, has just married another."

From under her purse, she pulled out a pop gun. She moved it slowly around in her hands so the whole class could see the roll of paper ammunition on a peg at the side of the gun. It was a pop gun, all right. I knew it shouldn't be in school.

"I am bereaved," she continued. "I cannot go on." She said this in the same sad voice. I felt so sorry for her.

Then she put the gun to her head and pulled the trigger. "Pouf," a small thread of smoke curled up. Miss Faucet, slowly, but with a final thump, fell on the floor. I didn't know if I should laugh or run for help. She got up after a few seconds and quickly wrote on the board, "obsessed."

"Who knows what this means?" she asked as if nothing had happened.

Benjie raised his hand. "It's like being haunted by an idea. You can't really help yourself."

"That's what I am, boys and girls—obsessed with Clark Gable, which causes me to do strange things like bringing a pop gun to class which *I know isn't allowed.*" She said the last words very loud and slow.

"Now let's get back to the important sentence."

She turned to the blackboard and wrote: "The love of my life, Clark Gable, has just married another."

"Who can tell me the action words of that sentence."

Quick as a lick, I raised my hand. I had never done that in school before.

"Yes, Karlan?"

"The action is, 'has married.' But the real action happened when you pulled the gun out and shot yourself and landed on the floor." I said that part fast.

"Your answer is correct, Karlan, but you should have stopped with 'married,' those other actions aren't written on the board." Her smile told me she liked what I'd said anyway.

I listened carefully and tried to stay quiet but then my legs began to twitch. They felt like they wanted to come right off and run away somewhere. Then I began itching—everywhere. The itching felt inside me, not where I could scratch. But I tried hard to find some place I could get at. I rubbed my back against the seat. I used my shoes to scrape my legs. My chewed-down nails worked on my arms. I stopped when I saw everyone looking at me. I stayed still as long as I could. Then, I stretched my legs straight in front of me to get the goobly jiggers out of them. Somehow I slipped off my chair, landing with a thump. Everyone laughed. Miss Faucet gave a look to the class that said, "none of that."

After class, she asked me to stay.

"Karlan, I can't keep shooting myself in the head and falling down to get your attention. What are we going to do about your restless behavior?"

"I'm sorry. I don't know what to do. I'm trying."

"I can see you are. But . . . ." She had that steely look again, her eye brows pulled together. Then she took a breath, smiled at me. "When I grew fast like you, my legs drove me crazy, too. But I can't have you disturb the other students."

I thought hard. I so wanted her to like me.

"I could sit way in the back," I looked at her hopefully, "where no one can see me." I pushed my shoulders up around my ears trying to think it out. "Then, maybe, when I can't stand my legs, I could get up and move around . . . really silent-like."

Miss Faucet watched me closely. She didn't smile but her eyes looked softer. All the deep ridges left her forehead.

"Let's give it a try."

"Oh, Miss Faucet," I said as I picked up my books. "You shouldn't point a gun at yourself or anyone else. My dad told me that."

"That's absolutely right, Karlan. But when you're acting a part, and it's a fake gun, it's okay."

The "back of the room" deal worked fine for a couple of days. Sometimes I lay on the floor and put my feet on the wall, arching my back. That felt wonderful.

But again Miss Faucet held me after class.

"We've got a problem, Karlan."

I interrupted fast. "I won't lie on the floor any more."

"No, that's not the problem. Benjie doesn't like you being alone in the back of the room. His mother called me. Benjie thinks you're being shunned. Do you know what that means?"

"No, Ma'am."

"It means deliberately avoiding someone, isolating a person."

"Did you tell Benjie's mother it was my idea?"

"Yes, of course. Even so, she said Benjie wants to sit with you. Would that be okay?"

"Sure. Benjie's the cutest boy in the whole school."

"Karlan, you will have to try harder to sit still. I don't want Benjie to miss my lessons because he's watching you. Okay?"

I nodded.

Benjie moved our desks so close no one could walk between them. Every day he brought a new joke or a cartoon for me. Most of them he drew himself. I didn't feel like wiggling around so much with Benjie right beside me.

"Karlie, if you listen carefully," Benjie told me, "you can catch the jokes Miss Faucet tells in her lesson."

I concentrated. Benjie was right. Miss Faucet had lots of hidden jokes. I felt proud if I laughed before the rest of the class. Benjie gave me a thumbs up.

It looked like school had stopped hating me.

# *Chapter Fourteen*

"Wait up," Mary Ann Miller called to me. I knew who she was because you couldn't help but notice her. She had long blond hair like Alice-in-Wonderland.

"Let's walk to school together," she said. "We live only a few blocks apart."

Things seemed to be getting better and better with Hampton Elementary School.

One day, Mary Ann told me about the blueberry pancakes her family planned for breakfast the next morning. I couldn't stop thinking about those pancakes. They would be wonderful with lots of maple syrup.

I woke up early and got dressed. I didn't have a plan, just an empty stomach. It was still dark when I walked to the Miller's house. I had trouble getting the gate opened. I knew the back door would be locked but I turned the knob hard anyway. It wouldn't budge. Next I stuck my head through the doggy door. I looked around the dark kitchen. The big clock gave an eerie green glow. It read 4:30.

As quietly as I could, I slipped through the doggy door, wiggling inch by inch. Gonzo, an old Irish Setter, needed lots of room. Maybe I could make it. Too late to change my mind, I lodged tight. I couldn't move. I heard a deep crack that sounded like the whole thing would fall apart. Just then I heard pat, pat, pat coming down the stairs. That sounded like Gonzo. He wouldn't be happy to see me plugging up his way to the out-of-doors.

"Please don't bark, Gonzo." I said it as loud as I could while whispering. I didn't want to wake anyone up. Gonzo pressed his nose into mine and began licking me. I had rubbed his belly a lot in the last few weeks. Mary Ann had brought me to her house after school for a snack and play time. Now Gonzo gave me the courage to try harder to get in. I twisted around getting on my back, my shoulders bent to my chest. With my legs braced against the outside step, I finally pushed my way through. Gonzo sniffed me all over.

Breaking into a house, even a friend's, tired me out. Gonzo put his head on my chest. We stayed that way. I listened to the silence of the house, breathing calmly again. Mary Ann said her mother always got up first. Everyone called Mrs. Miller, "Bunny."

"That's a ridiculous name for a grown woman with an important husband," mother had said. I didn't like the sound of that, his being important. Maybe he'd be mean.

Mrs. Miller didn't scare me at all. She seemed like my Aunt Lenore, always smiling at me. She let Mary Ann and me dress up in her good clothes. She even let me wear her gold hostess gown with feathers on the bottom.

"Now that, Karlan, is your color." She stood back, her head to one side admiring me.

I couldn't wait to be grown up. I'd buy everything in gold. I felt like a butterfly being born out of something brown and old. Being in the Miller's house felt like that. Of course no one had invited me to come over at 4:30 in the morning and almost break Gonzo's door.

Maybe if I set the table, the Millers wouldn't mind my breaking in. I carefully opened the silverware drawer, making sure nothing rattled. I found napkins and then quietly looked in the fridge to see if they drank orange juice. I stared at the food. All at once, I heard a deep voice right behind me.

"Good morning. It's—uh—Karlan, isn't it?"

I jumped so hard I hit the mayonnaise jar. It almost fell out, but I caught it.

"Good reflexes," said the voice, then he flicked on the kitchen light. "To what do we owe the pleasure of your company at five in the morning?"

Mr. Miller didn't look like an important man. His bathrobe could have been a washed out old rug. His blond hair stuck up all over the place. But his eyes smiled at me, waiting for me to say something. I couldn't make my mouth move.

"I know who you are, Karlan, because Bunny pointed you out to me when you were riding your bicycle by our house the other day." He spoke slowly then waited. His soft voice lulled me.

"I—I—well, actually, Mr. Miller," words finally worked their way through my chattering teeth. "I got here at four-thirty and played with Gonzo."

He looked at me closely. "Karlan, is there something wrong at home? Are you ill?"

"Oh, nothing like that. It's just that Mary Ann said you were having blueberry pancakes for breakfast and it's all I could think of since the moment she told me. See, last night we had milk-toast and I couldn't get those pancakes out of . . . ."

"Back up there, Karlan. What's 'milk-toast?'"

"That's when my dad's out of town and my mother has a headache. She makes toast, puts it in a cereal bowl and pours warm milk over it. Actually, I hate milk-toast but I hate other things more like lima beans or pabulum."

"It's a good thing you came over, Karlan. Headaches must be contagious. Bunny has one too. I planned to put out cereal but those blueberry pancakes sound wonderful."

Mr. Miller stuck his head in the refrigerator and began handing me things. I worked alongside him, rinsing off the berries, breaking open eggs. Pretty soon morning sunlight moved across the room.

"Hey, look at this, Karlan. I found bacon in the back of the refrigerator. Probably meant for Sunday but since we're at it, let's do this breakfast up right."

He smiled happily at me.

The bacon sizzled. We placed everything on the table. Mr. Miller even had me pour maple syrup into a little pitcher, then put it in a pan of hot water. I never heard of doing that. It seemed fancy, like a restaurant.

"Karlie, Karlie, Karlie," screamed Mary Ann, running into the room. "When did you get here?" Her face looked so full of happiness, I started to jump up and down.

Mr. Miller said, "Careful now. I want Bunny to sleep in. I think I'll bring her up some coffee."

"Don't bother. The smell of that bacon tore away my headache." Bunny came down the stairs wearing the gold hostess gown. She looked beautiful. Then she saw me.

"Karlan, I thought I heard your laugh."

"Oh, I hope you don't mind, Bunny," Mr. Miller said smoothly. "I invited Karlan over for breakfast. I needed a helper and she came to the rescue. We've had a splendid time."

"What a clever man you are," said Bunny. "I'm going to have to have headaches more often."

I don't remember a better breakfast. As Mr. Miller was leaving for his important job, he came over to me.

"I'll show you where the back door key is hidden, Karlan. I hope you'll come for breakfast often."

I did.

# *Chapter Fifteen*

The dining room table looked ready for a party. Joan and I had no idea why. We looked at the flowers father had brought and mother had arranged. Ula, our cook, had been working all day. She didn't know anything either.

"I'm just making what Mrs. Richards said."

"Put on your Sunday best and be at the table at six sharp." Mother said it with a smile. I could tell she liked being mysterious. Maybe we were going on a long trip. Maybe father got a big raise.

Morgan got an upset stomach. That happened to him when there was too much tension or excitement. He lay on the floor moaning. I rubbed his back until he felt better. Finally we all gathered around the table waiting for the announcement.

Father cleared his throat. "I have wonderful news." He paused so long Joan and I couldn't hold our breath any longer. "Your mother is going to have a baby."

Joan grabbed my arm. We both went cold. How could father be happy? Mother smiled at us as if she didn't mind at all. Had she forgotten what happened the last time?

"It's important that you help your mother all you can so she doesn't get overly tired."

Father looked hard at me. I knew what he meant. I fought with my mother. Joan never did. She cried when mother called her a name. Joan didn't know how to be mean. But I did. Once I put all of mother's best underwear in the toilet. That happened after mother yelled at Joan for nothing. If mother looked like she wanted to hit me, I stuck my elbows out and she got hurt. If she called me a bad name, I put a dead mouse in her drawer. I drew pictures of witches and wrote, "U," and stuck them in her purse where she would be sure to find them.

Mother never said a word about what I did. Instead, she'd ask me to have "tea" with her. No one else got invited to these tea and cinnamon toast parties. Momma read my fortune in the leaves. She said I had a good heart and would soon stop making her sad. At the end, she always told me the same thing. "Someday a tall, dark, handsome man with flashing eyes will love you. He'll make all your pain go away and fill your heart with joy."

Then I would read her tea leaves. I made up great adventures for her like seeing four sunsets at once full of colors so strong they could pick her up and carry her all the way to Paris.

"Remember, mother, you told us that's where you left a big chunk of your heart."

I went away from our tea parties full of good feelings for mother. We'd be happy with each other for a few weeks, then bad stuff would bubble up like a witch's brew and it would start all over again.

The other time we had peace together was when we visited Lac Simon in French Canada. We went for three summers in a row. Even Ula came with us. With nothing to do but swim and explore, we stayed gentle with each other. We didn't have running water or electricity, just a hunk of ice to keep our food cold. Maybe because we lived with the earth, we got along.

Mother got up early to watch the sun rise. I would follow close behind and sit with her. We didn't talk, just looked at the awakening sky. During those times, I wondered why I'd ever been so angry with her.

Joan and I talked it over the night after the big party. We would have to do more to help.

"It's up to you, Karlan, to take care of Morgan and keep him out of trouble. I'll do more housework and help Ula with cooking and doing the dishes."

I didn't promise but I tried harder to keep track of my wild brother. I vowed to stop my war on our mother.


Father decided the best way to take care of mother during her pregnancy would be a trip to Paris. The war had ended. They had lots of friends to see. The happy part of the news came when he told me Miss Faucet would live with us for the six weeks while they traveled.

"Maybe she can teach you to read," he said hopefully.

Morgan went to Aunt Lenore. That turned me into the baby of the house again. I liked that. Ula left us to get married. Miss Faucet didn't mind doing the cooking. I helped. She taught me all her secrets. We had hot chocolate with marshmallows every day after school. We made huge dinners together and yummy desserts. Miss Painter came over on the weekends. We had parties and played games together.

Miss Faucet didn't help me much with school work but she read to me. I sat on her lap. My long legs hung way over the chair but I didn't care. I couldn't get enough of her holding me.

# *Chapter Sixteen*

Mother stayed in the hospital a long time after our new baby was born. Mrs. Olson came to replace Ula but she couldn't come until the day after mother got home. That meant Joan and I had lots of work to do. We scrubbed the house cleaner than it had ever been. Joan did most of it. I gathered brightly colored weeds and put them into mother's crystal vases.

"She won't like that," Joan warned.

When mother walked in the door, she didn't say anything about the clean house. She started sneezing.

"Get those weeds out of here."

Joan and I burst out laughing. Mother had no idea what we found so funny. I couldn't be happier. Our momma seemed her old self. And my new baby brother, Bob, stole my heart.

I wanted a special celebration at Christmas. I wanted to get everyone gifts that would make them stand up and shout, "hip-hip-hooray." Most of all, I wanted something special for baby Bob. I decided to get my gifts from Hudson's Department Store.

Since I didn't have money, just big ideas, I left the house planning to shoplift. I didn't think about what Miss Faucet or Miss Painter would say. I absolutely knew I shouldn't steal. Lynn would never do such a thing. Bob

Andrew might be a hellion but he wouldn't shoplift. But I'm doing this for the family, I told myself. I'm going to make people happy.

I wore Joan's old coat. Mother had picked it up at the church goodwill bazaar. Joan wore it for years. The green color looked like leaves crushed by muddy boots. A person could disappear in a coat like that. No one would see me. I'd pick up little, but wonderful, gifts.

The strange thing about our Christmas celebrations was that mother often forgot to buy us presents. I think she planned to but the days would slip by and suddenly there stood Christmas Eve smack dab in front of her.

"I can't go out," she complained. "It's too crowded and snowy. I'll never recover to enjoy Christmas day."

She did buy gifts for aunts, uncles, and all their kids. She did that early. She planned to find special presents for us later when they went on sale just before Christmas. She told me all about her good intentions. I believed her. On Christmas Eve I even helped her find presents to give, like her old purse for Joan or my crayons for Morgan. I didn't want that this year. I decided I should be the Christmas hero.

My adventure began two weeks before the big day. I took what money dad had on his bureau and headed out into the cold. Dad expected this loot to be taken. He didn't give allowances, just put his change out for Joan and me to share. Morgan didn't know about the ever-bubbling money machine in my parents' room. In another year, he'd be part of the split. As for Hal, he always had a job and probably never touched dad's money. Besides, Hal wouldn't get home until just before Christmas. He went to college now.

I took the bus to Hudson's Department Store, which meant a half hour ride. I loved all parts of the day, the crowded bus with its strange smells, the drippy slushy weather, even the ice water finding its way into my boots. I knew Hudson's would be steamy warm with crowds of laughing, hurrying shoppers. I could hardly wait as I bounced along in the bus, planning, feeling the butterflies in my stomach, but knowing I'd succeed.

I overheard my mother tell Aunt Lenore she needed pink leather gloves for her new outfit. She couldn't find them anywhere. Hudson's would have them, I just knew it. Sure enough, I spotted pink gloves on the middle shelf. I waited patiently until a lady in a red coat asked the busy clerk if she could try on the pink gloves, the only pair left. My heart beat fast as the lady examined them, then put them aside. Whew! Fast as a lizard, my hand went up and the gloves went down my blouse.

Hal's present took no time. He lost his Swiss army knife. I walked by the display, spotted the knife, and without changing my speed, it slipped into my pocket. I didn't turn my head, just my eyes. No doubt about it, I was a natural pro.

My father just got handkerchiefs, easy to lift.

I knew what I wanted for Morgan, a pair of handcuffs. He'd love them but I might end up being his prisoner. I'd pick them up in the toy department.

Joan presented a problem. I had stolen a gift for her birthday. My first time to shoplift and she spoiled it. It had been so easy, but she knew I didn't have enough money for the necklace and she wouldn't have anything to do with it. So I would have to make something for her. But I could count on her not giving me away. She never tattled.

Now I had to find that very special, wonderful gift for our new baby. I wanted something not just good but sensational. I planned on telling Bobby over and over again, "This came from your wonderful sister, Karlan. You adore your sister Karlan more than anyone else on earth." This gift would make me his favorite. But what?

I saw it the moment I entered the toy department. It stood by itself in the corner—a huge brown bear. I decided to break all my rules about being a clever thief. I walked right up to the bear, picked him up and headed for Santa Claus sitting on his throne. A long line of excited kids waited their turn. Parents stood near. The crowd felt thick and alive with holiday magic.

"The best Christmas ever, Santa Claus," I shouted over the voices. "This is for my baby brother."

"Ho, ho, ho," said Santa. "What a good sister you are. Now wait in line for your turn."

Parents and kids looked at me and smiled. I didn't blend into the wall. I became a number one attraction. I played it up big. Casually, I walked up to the counter where I saw the handcuffs. Using the bear as a shield, I slipped a pair into my coat pocket.

"Merry Christmas," I shouted with a huge smile on my face. I gave out holiday greetings all through the store and walked out to the bus.

I could hardly wait for my day of giving. My heart pounded. I felt sick with anticipation. It turned out better than I imagined. Mother beamed when she opened her package. "Perfect, perfect, oh, you sweet child, how did you ever know . . . and the right size too . . . magnificent color." Mother positively glowed.

Dad liked his white handkerchiefs.

Hal studied me as he looked over his knife. "Is this the one I lost?" he asked.

I gave "the shrug."

Just as I expected, Morgan jumped up and down when he saw the handcuffs.

Joan smiled at me when she unwrapped a candy box I had covered with stickers for her hairpins. Now they wouldn't be all over our bathroom drawer.

The big finale came when I opened the closet door and brought out my Teddy Bear. I heard the audible "ahh" and got goose bumps.

"I didn't know they made them that big," said my dad. He looked confused. Maybe he wondered how I could afford such gifts. I knew he'd forget to ask mother about it.

Baby Bob crawled right over. I got down on all fours and slid along with him. "This gift is from me," I said, "your wonderful sister Karlan." I put my face next to his soft cheek. "You love your sister Karlan," I whispered.

After everyone got over their surprise, we hustled to go to Aunt Lenore and Uncle George's house for more presents and Christmas dinner. Dad and I got in one car with Morgan, Hal, and Bob. Joan and mom went in our other car. This had become a tradition because mother never got ready on time.

Once we got to Aunt Lenore's house, Lynn and I chased each other around, hugging and laughing. I felt ten feet tall and didn't mind the long wait for mother.

"Let's get started," said Lenore. "There's no telling how long that sister of mine will be."

Just then, the door swung open and mother and Joan walked in. Mother carried Teddy. Lenore and all the cousins "oohed" in delight. Lenore had a new baby too. Baby Mitt had been born just after my brother, Bob. Mother made a big deal of giving Mitt my Teddy Bear.

"I couldn't resist," she said. "I wanted something outstanding for your new baby, Lenore."

Mother didn't look at me. I stood frozen. I felt too miserable to cry.

Joan tried to hug me. "Sorry Karlan." She slowly rubbed my back. "Mom forgot to buy a present for Mitt." Joan looked around to make sure no one was listening. "She grabbed your Teddy Bear. I heard her say, 'thank goodness' under her breath. I couldn't stop her." Joan sighed.

I looked at the floor. It felt like I lived inside a book or something. Nothing seemed real. Joan bent down to hear what I said.

My voice came out small. "I didn't know you were allowed to steal Christmas."

# *Chapter Seventeen*

Every kid who attended my elementary school dreamed of being the top student. Starting in kindergarten parents pushed their children because they knew that the Hampton valedictorian had it made for life. The honor, of course, went to the student with the best grades. I didn't have a chance, being third from the bottom. But it didn't matter. Benjie had it sewed up for years. Everyone knew that. I planned to congratulate him. We had only another four weeks before the end of school so I better do it soon.

Miss Faucet asked me to stay after school. She did that a lot.

"We're going to celebrate," she said.

Our last celebration happened when I had almost spelled "telephone" in the spelling bee. I had missed only the middle "e." Miss Faucet said we should enjoy each little triumph.

We went to our favorite ice cream parlor with the red checkered tablecloths and the white metal chairs. I started to order my usual chocolate milk shake when Miss Faucet stopped me.

"This is too exciting for just a milk shake. Have a banana split."

What had I done? I had handed in my homework as always and it had come back with lots of red marks as always. I looked at her and waited.

"I've talked to Benjie and his parents." She paused for a long time just smiling at me. "He's giving up his place as valedictorian so you can speak at graduation."

"Me? Benjie's the best and what about all the kids ahead of me?"

"I'll handle that," Miss Faucet took my hand. "You just need a little push so you'll feel like the winner you are. Benjie says you'll give a great speech. He wants you to do this."

The next day, I asked Benjie.

"You're the best person for the job," he said.

He looked happy about it.

I started to get excited. I stood up straighter. I smiled at the other students. I also got worried. What could I say to all those parents and those super smart kids? I didn't want anyone laughing at me. But I did want to figure out my own speech. Benjie and Miss Faucet believed in me.

I heard a story on the radio I thought I could use for my speech. It told of a wandering boy who came to a farm hoping for work. Because he had a skinny body and a dreamy look, the farmer couldn't decide if he should hire him.

"Oh, well," said the farmer, "I'm desperate for a helper."

After a few weeks, the farmer complained to his wife. "I made a mistake. See what he's doing now? He works steady enough but then looks off at the hills, smiling, always cheerful." The farmer shook his head. "With everything that has to be done around here, no one should be that happy."

The boy did seem to enjoy each day. He didn't make a show of doing all the little jobs like tightening the hinges on the barn door or getting the feed in before it rained. All that stuff just got done.

I named my speech, *Sleeping when the Wind Blows*. The point of the story was that when the wind howled, the helper could sleep like a baby because everything had been taken care of. And, most important, he had enjoyed himself in the process.

I made my story mysterious, exciting, while trying to say something worthwhile. Aunt Lenore helped me put drama in it with just the right pauses. Lenore had been an actress before she married George so she knew all about that stuff. This had a chance of working out. Only one thing left: find a dress.

Miss Faucet sent home a note telling the girls to wear pastels for graduation and the boys to be in dark trousers with white shirts.

As soon as mother and I walked into the dress shop I got worried. There was a big sign: *SALE: 50% OFF.* I prayed there would be a pastel dress in my size because I knew my mother. She couldn't resist a bargain. I thought of what Miss Faucet had said about being "obsessed." That described my mother when it came to saving money. She couldn't control herself. A good sale blinded her.

She went through all the dresses on the rack in about two minutes. Then she began slowly looking at one after another. I stood back. Finally, she stopped and pulled out an expensive looking taffeta creation. The color? Black.

"Mother, no. I have to wear a light shade."

"You are the honoree. You can wear whatever you want. Look at this dress. It's so well made. The material is unbelievable. It will wear like iron. You'll have this dress when you go to college and the store's almost giving it away." She said that last part in a whisper as if afraid the store manager would grab it right out of her hands.

"It's *black*, mother."

"Not completely. It has these rich-looking gun metal stripes in velvet."

"It's too old for me. It's on sale because it's a winter dress, not spring. I don't like it."

"Nonsense, try it on. If it doesn't fit, we'll go someplace else."

It fit so perfectly I could hardly walk in the tight skirt. I knew when I had been defeated. I didn't want to fight about my big day. Perhaps mother had it right. I could wear a different color as the speaker, sort of like appearing in a tux.

When I entered the school auditorium, Miss Painter and Miss Faucet waited at the door for me. They even brought me a corsage. Miss Painter took one look at my dress and burst into tears.

"Your mother did this."

Miss Faucet tried to hush her. I knew neither of them liked my mother. It made me sad. I felt protective of my momma. I could be mad as all get out at her but I didn't want anyone else saying mean things. I loved Miss Faucet and Miss Painter but I couldn't let them be critical of my mother. I never talked against her to anyone but Joan. Besides, she didn't deserve it this time. I took a deep breath and tried to explain.

"I know this isn't what you wanted me to wear but the reason mother bought it is because it will wear like iron and we got it on sale. She really, truly wants me to look nice. See, it does fit perfectly."

Neither of them said anything more.

I pushed the dress out of my mind. I felt confident when I stood up at the podium. This seemed like church with all the smiling faces looking at me. I'd entertain them.

I went through the whole twenty minute speech just like Lenore and I had practiced. When I got to the end, my stomach dropped. I knew I had it wrong. No one could sleep if a terrible storm came. My speech didn't make sense.

I raised my voice and went on.

"But you can only sleep through ordinary winds in life. What can you do if the wind is huge, like a tornado? Then . . . ." Everyone waited for the final words. I had no idea how to end. I felt so afraid of wind, it made me sick when it whipped through the trees. I thought the world would blow apart. Why did I pick a story about wind? I had to say something.

"Then . . . ." I slowly looked over the audience. I wanted them to think I knew what came next. But I still couldn't figure out how to close. People probably expected me to say something about believing in God and putting my hand into His. No way could I say that because I felt all mixed up about God. I took a deep breath.

"Then—you have to reach inside yourself and—and find the strength you never knew you had."

The clapping came like thunder, long and hard. I felt sky high.

"You really made that dramatic," said Miss Faucet.

"Good for you," said Lenore. "Did we practice that ending?"

I just smiled.

Benjie gave me an awkward hug. "You were great and you look so, well, so sophisticated." I didn't know for sure what that meant but he said it sweetly.

My parents worked their way through the crowd. My father's whispered words were loud enough for me to hear.

"Elsie, what could you have been thinking? Our twelve-year-old looks twenty-five and—and—like a woman of the evening."

Mother's face turned bright red. Father never criticized her. She rushed out of the auditorium.

I never saw my black dress again.

# Chapter Eighteen

It started when I climbed the outside grill of a large building under construction. I scrambled over the high fence, ignored the "no trespassing" sign, started up—all on a dare. When I got to the third level and looked down, panic got me. I closed my eyes hoping the dizziness would pass. My left foot felt secure but that was all. My right hand held on to a slick metal pole. Once I started sweating, my grip began to slip. My other hand found only air. I moved my right foot in circles searching for a safe perch. Nothing—only space. Then I wet my pants.

A dark-skinned guy climbing up to help me yelled, "Hey, have a little pity. I'm on your side."

He joked about the "waterworks" while he guided me down. He made me laugh. I forgot my panic. I looked around for my friends. They had disappeared. This sweet fellow—a couple of years older than me—had saved me from falling. I wanted to hug him but I didn't. When he walked me home, both my parents happened to be standing on the front lawn. Neither said anything, not even about my smelly clothes. About a week later, they asked how many Negroes were in my class. I had never considered my parents prejudiced. The question surprised me.

Six months later, we had one of mother's "special" dinner parties. I hoped she wouldn't announce a new baby coming. Joan had left for Paris to study French for several months, so she couldn't be my ally. Hal had gone on a Mormon mission. Morgan had a stomach ache—again. Baby Bobby, always a good kid, sat quietly waiting. Finally, mother made the announcement: "We have a new home."

"What?" I was the only one to be upset. "Why do we have to move? This house is big enough. Mary Ann lives just two blocks away and Lynn . . . Lynn's close. Please, I feel good here."

Mother looked at me calmly. "Remember, Karlan, when we watched the sun rise at Lac Simone?" Her face looked radiant. "That's the feeling you'll have when you see this house."

"Is this about Negroes being in my school?"

My parents ignored the question.

"Wait until you see it," said my father. "And, and . . . there's enough land so I can grow vegetables. I miss being a farmer. Those are my roots." He looked over at mother with the same excitement in his face.

I knew there wasn't any point arguing.


It wasn't the house that spoke to me but the land. Our new home on Lone Pine Road didn't have a sidewalk or a paved street. We lived on a rutted dirt lane. That felt romantic. We were in the country all right. Trees everywhere, no cars, no noise, just birds. A little pond sat between our home and the neighbors, but the houses were so far apart, we seemed alone.

I walked slowly, dragging my feet through the golden leaves. I wandered for a long time, feeling what? Feeling a sense of belonging. I wouldn't get lost in this nurturing place. It welcomed me. The trees bent toward me as if they'd been waiting.

I went through the house room by room. They were large with tall windows that pulled in the sun. Everywhere I looked, open space, quiet. Mother even had her own study so she could write poetry in peace. Good things had happened in this house. I felt the spirit in it.

No one said anything to me. They didn't have to. All of us sensed a contentment and a gladness for each other.

Mother . . . mother needed this home. And so did I.

# *Chapter Nineteen*

I walked the mile and a half to my new school, Hillcrest. I didn't want mother with me. I needed to do this alone but I sure felt nervous. I took deep breaths to keep the nausea under control. Despite everything Miss Faucet had done for me, I still felt like an alien who would wither in anything called a "school."

I knocked on the principal's door. The sign said "Mr. Spiess."

"Come in," a deep voice called, sounding like it might break into song.

The principal beamed up at me from his chair. When he realized a new student stood before him, he rose to his feet, extending his hand. I liked him right away. He had a gold tooth in the front that made him look dashing despite his balding head. His round tinted glasses set off a warm face.

"I'm—a—Karlan Richards. We just moved here from Detroit. I went to Hampton, then Mumford. I've come to register—to be an eighth grader here."

"Karlan . . . Karlan Richards, Hampton Elementary. Why does that sound familiar?"

"I got to be valedictorian. You probably read it in the school paper that gets sent around."

"Good for you, Karlan. Looks like we have a scholar."

"Oh, no—no, Mr. Spiess, nothing of the sort. You don't understand. It's all Miss Faucet's fault. She gave me this—this undeserved reputation. The same thing happened when I started Mumford. That school put me into advanced classes. The poor teachers thought they messed up when . . . ."

"Miss Faucet's famous," he interrupted. "I'm sure she knew what she was doing. I won't let her down." Mr. Spiess squinted, looking at me carefully.

"You say you're in the eighth grade? You don't look like an eighth grader. More like a high school junior."

"I flunked first grade. I guess that's hard to do."

"Well, we'll right that wrong. You are now a ninth grader."

I wiggled my shoulders in pleasure, feeling years older, pleased with the world.

While Mr. Spiess filled in my papers, I scanned the bulletin board. My eyes brightened even more when I spotted a notice.

"You need someone to clean up and wash tables in the cafeteria," I said. "Fifty cents a day and all you can eat? Sounds good to me."

"You'd want to do that?" Mr. Spiess looked surprised.

"I could eat all the time," I confessed.

"Wouldn't you rather sit out in the sun during recess with the other girls? You'll like them," he told me. "They're a special group in the ninth grade."

And they were. "Wolfie" and "Lucky" and all the rest became marvelous friends but I never gave up my cafeteria job. I learned a secret. The cooks brought special dishes just for the crew. I ate like a queen and got paid for it.

That first day, I longed to tell Mr. Spiess that a brilliant light-filled energy surrounded him but I knew better than to do that. I let the good feelings roll over me, knowing I was lucky to have him in my life.

# Chapter Twenty

No sound woke me. I sat up to total stillness. Everything had changed in a few dark hours. I knew snow but this oblivion took my breath away. I put my hand against my dormer window. I studied the delicately stacked flakes that half-blinded my view. Our young fruit trees drooped like worn out peasants with heavy loads. I couldn't find a familiar bush anywhere, just huge toadstool-looking mounds. A fairy tale, a wonderment. And I sure wouldn't want to be out in the middle of it.

One good thing, big snow meant no school. I crawled back into the warmth of my bed and fell deeply asleep.

"Get up, quick. I need your help." Mother shook me awake. I sat up so fast I got dizzy.

"What? What?" I looked at her determined face.

"The silly bus driver got stuck. He thinks he can dump fifteen wet students in my house. Imagine the mess they'll make. We're going to walk them to school."

I sat on the edge of my bed trying to make sense of her plan.

"Ah, mother, the bus got stuck because the conditions are impossible. You can't expect kids to walk to school."

"It will be good for them. See, the snow's letting up." She stood at the window, ignoring me. "Hurry up, will you? I want you to take up the rear and make sure no one falls into a snow bank."

I had only been at my new school a year. I wanted to make a good impression. This would let everyone know that our family was weird.

Mother had packed the kids into our cold garage. No one said a word when I walked in. Ouch. There stood two senior boys I had had an eye on. I wanted to crawl under our car.

"I'll just hike home from here," said one of them.

"I'm sorry about this." I could feel my red face. "But could you help me get these kids to school? I think it'll be easier for parents to pick them up there, don't you?"

I waited. No one said anything.

"The streets will be plowed at the school first." I kept scrambling for something to make mother's forced march not too outrageous. "I'll bet there are other stranded buses." I began to sound lame even to myself.

"Yeah," said a little kid, his teeth chattering. "Bet they landed at a house where the mother made hot chocolate and treated them nice."

"Yeah", mumbled the other kids.

Just then mother appeared in a warm coat, boots and a fur cap. She waved us out like a general on a special mission. Everyone followed obediently.

The wind had picked up, whipping snow into our faces. We sank down with each step. The little kids seemed to be swimming. Their arms churned the snow to propel them forward. I counted heads. The older boys stayed to help.

I looked around at all the kids struggling and couldn't help but laugh. It seemed too ridiculous. We would be known for all history as the party who disappeared in the great whiteout. How would we explain this to the police? Surely, parents would complain. I didn't know what law we were breaking, but endangering minors came to mind. The older guys took up the laughter and started throwing snow balls. Smaller kids wouldn't be left out. They deliberately buried themselves. Mother marched on, keeping a fast pace. She probably couldn't hear us over the sound of the wind.

We got ourselves under control but something changed. One of the girls began singing, "*How Many Bottles of Beer on the Wall.*" This went on until we started walking like drunks, falling into drifts and being outrageous. We tried leapfrogging over snowdrifts. Usually we ended up falling on our faces. No one cared.

Polly, a vivacious twelve-year-old, decided to make an angel. She carefully placed herself on the soft new snow and sank.

"Too bad, we've lost Polly," one of the seniors announced. We looked down. Polly smiled happily up at us. We dragged her out. About this time, I noticed the wind had died down. With all our antics, we grew warm, unzipping our coats.

We came around the corner of the school, a gaggly clump of happy chaos. Mother dutifully stood waiting for us on the school porch. Mr. Spiess stood at her side.

"Karlan promised us hot chocolate with marshmallows," screamed one of the students. "Yeah," echoed the other kids.

"She knows the cafeteria better than I do," said the principal.

Mother stood looking both smug and vindicated.

# *Chapter Twenty-One*

My hero, Bob Andrew, continued to help me with reading. Other than that, he paid no attention to me until the church service ended. Then he would chase me all over the yard and tackle me. We wrestled in the grass, tumbling over and over. I loved it.

Once, when I was about ten, he grabbed at my hair and quickly pulled away. "It's all tangled," he said. He made it sound like something yucky. "You don't comb your hair right."

Punching him sounded good to me. "I brush the top layer," I said it with attitude. "The underneath part is my business, Bob Andrew."

The next Sunday my hair was shiny clean, snarl-free. He ran his hands through it, but gently. It made my heart pound.

We decided to go steady when I turned fourteen.

The Andrew twins were known as hellions. They used their identical looks to play tricks on their teachers, even the church elders. They had a worse reputation than I did. Then they grew up.

"I guess I'm mellowing," Bob told me. "Mother isn't leaving the dinner table in tears any more."

Something important got lost for me. Bob became one of "them," a good citizen. I began to feel lonely even when we were together.

The twins grew into tall, handsome young men with straight blond hair and hazel-green eyes. All five boys in the family turned heads.

Chad, Bob's twin, rarely spoke to me. I knew I had caused trouble for the brothers. Bob and I used their new Ford almost every weekend. They had bought the car to be shared. Chad scowled when he passed me. Bob never talked about difficulties with Chad or how their relationship had changed. He only talked of the joy they shared with music and ideas.

One Sunday after church, I sat waiting in the grass for Bob. It was Chad who turned the corner, surprised to see me. I was Bob's first girlfriend. That had to be hard on Chad who seemed more shy than his twin.

"Karlan," he said my name slowly as if trying to get used to it. "I just wondered about—what you talk about—with my brother, I mean. Do you, do you have any goals? You know, things you want to do with your life? I don't understand who you are."

Chad's loneliness didn't hit me until that moment. I didn't like his question about "goals" but I heard his confusion. He had lost part of his twin to someone who didn't make sense to him.

"I don't have goals like you and Bob." I squinted up at Chad. He moved to block the sun from my eyes. "I try to get through each day. Sometimes that's hard. And, by the way, that's what we talk about, a lot, my not having direction." He still didn't sit down. "I hope, though, that like you, I would block the sun from blinding the person in front of me."

When I looked at Chad I saw Bob's image but entirely different eyes looked down at me. I also saw his pain.

"I hurt too, Chad, but for different reasons." That was all I could think to say. He walked away. We rarely spoke again. But he didn't scowl anymore when he passed me.

I didn't tell Bob about my hallucinations or auras. My panic attacks never happened with him. Only Joan knew some of my secrets. To the rest of the world, I shared the surface of me. I walled off so many things, I felt like a stranger in my own skin.

How could I tell Bob or anyone else that my "project" dealt with uncovering demons rattling around in my head ready to spring loose. My long walks in our woods usually ended in my pressing into a friendly tree. I'd let myself be absorbed and flow out more whole. Who could I tell that to?


In high school, Bob and I made out for hours, tucked away on a dark dirt road, snug in his new Ford. I never worried about our going too far. Bob wouldn't let that happen. I flowed in the safety of his being in charge. He'd gasp sometimes, even cry. I slipped into peace with him and let myself drift away.

"I don't mind you falling asleep in my arms," Bob complained, "but do you have to snore?"

Poor guy. I couldn't tell him why I felt so exhausted, why I couldn't sleep in my own bed. Why I wandered through our house looking for safety. I kept secrets piled on top of each other.

"I feel safe with you, Bob. I can sleep in your arms. I wish you knew how important that is to me."

"Well, I'm glad one of us is happy." He sighed but hugged me close anyway.

When Bob and I attended concerts, I'd let myself fall into a kind of suspended semi-awareness. I let the music take me away. He saw my rapture as appreciation for what mattered so much to him. Bob took piano lessons seriously, even thought of a concert career.

He also wanted to be a physician and own his own plane so he could treat patients in remote areas. Bob seemed emotionally organized. I hated it. I felt fragmented and isolated. We went steady through most of high school. Our battles were hot and frequent but we never broke up.

One Saturday he announced we would go on a picnic. It came across like an order. He had an agenda. I saw heaviness in his face.

"I want us to be completely alone," he said with great seriousness. "For once, I want to talk something through."

I knew what he wanted. This would be breakup time.

We got settled by a small lake. I brought the sandwiches. He brought fruit and cold apple juice. His mother contributed brownies. I fussed with the ants invading our food, twigs biting through our picnic blanket. I didn't want to be in this place. This was a fight I wanted no part of. I tried to plan what I'd say. Bob broke through.

"I've considered this for a long time, Karlan. You know I love you. I think we have a future together." It sounded memorized.

"I've thought about what really matters to me," he went on. "The church comes first, then my country. I love my family but you come before any of them. You're third in my priorities."

Ugh!

He stopped, waiting for a response. The Mormon Church meant the most to him? I couldn't grasp it. We never talked about religion. If I told him the church didn't even figure in my world, our relationship would end. I searched for something to say. I didn't want to mention Mormonism. I could never explain how empty it left me. A blast of hot anger grabbed me, took me by surprise. I jumped up from our blanket, lashed out at him.

"Why should you love the United States? What's wrong with caring for—for—France or—Canada? What about Africa? Lots of people live in Africa. They're important too, you know."

My confused feelings groped for words.

"I don't like you isolating yourself as an American, Bob Andrew. And—and—telling me I'm lucky to be third." I screamed the last part while throwing my half-eaten brownie in his face.

Bob looked amazed but not angry.

"I just told you, you mean more to me than anyone and you're mad, you're mad, because I happen to love my country? Your problem is you don't commit to anything."

After that confrontation, I felt dishonest. Bob would never accept a Mormon doubter. I truly cared for him, more than I wanted to admit. My family loved him. But we didn't have a chance together.

"You could do a lot worse than Bob Andrew," my mother told me.

She gave my impassive face a long look. "We'll give you the Steinway as a wedding present."

I didn't argue. I'd let things go on until Bob went to college. He had a year up on me. Separation would create a graceful ending. Until then I'd enjoy the concerts.

# *Chapter Twenty-Two*

It took four months for me to land back in the principal's office—this time the door read, "Dean of Students."

There had been no question where I'd go to college. The Brigham Young University represented my parent's last hope. Maybe some good Mormon boy would do what they couldn't—make me into a believer.

Within a week of my arrival, I presented myself to the Student Extension office.

"I'm an entertainer," I told the audition committee. "Let me do one-person skits or readings. I don't want to perform on campus but, you know, for outside groups, like Chamber of Commerce, senior citizens." I smiled at the three strangers looking at me. "Older people think I'm funny."

"Let's hear what you got." An attractive woman with a Hollywood look waved me on stage.

They listened. They laughed. I felt the warm rush that came with fitting in.

Dorothy Parker's "The Telephone Call" became my favorite reading. I hammed it up. The story involved a conversation with God, first pleading, then cursing Him. I figured my profanity got me the invitation to the Dean of Students.

I knocked on his door.

A stern, middle aged man with undisciplined hair around his ears gave me the once over. I wouldn't get a laugh out of him. He examined my folder. I saw my smiling face on the front of the packet. Pretty good picture for once.

"You give readings." He looked at me without a trace of a smile. "You go out to the public as a representative of our Church and our University and curse God."

Oh, oh. My stomach dropped.

"I'm doing Dorothy Parker's work. The words aren't mine. She writes about feelings that are, well, universal. They might happen to anyone, the feelings, I mean. That's, that's what makes her funny."

"How many of these, 'presentations,' have you given?"

"Oh, three . . . five . . . I could do something else."

"Your grades suggest you should spend your time studying."

I nodded. I barely had a passing grade in two of my classes. Another one was stuck on "D." I gave a sigh of relief. I'd been worried about *The Book of Mormon* teacher telling on me. I had only suggested the possibility that . . . .

"You asked in class if Joseph Smith might have had hallucinations. Were you trying to entertain the students?" Now he sounded angry.

"No, I, it came out because—when the teacher said there could be no other explanation . . . ."

"You confuse me, Miss Richards. You come from a devout Mormon family with all the advantages but you make a joke of our religion."

Silence. I let it drag on. I couldn't think what to say.

I thought he might be done with me. But he kept looking at my folder, then looking at me again. I sat still, trying to appear contrite. I didn't want to be sent home. I loved my roommates. I enjoyed my freedom. Some of my classes—psychology, theater—I found exciting.

I began to think the Dean would never let me leave. He answered the phone, picked up another student's folder, put down the phone. Every once in a while, he looked over at me.

"You didn't have to take an entrance exam, did you?" he leaned toward me.

"No . . . ."

"That's what I thought. We give the children of good Mormon families a try at higher education. But sometimes it means students who aren't ready for college come to our campus and cause problems."

Oh boy, here it came. I'd be sent home in disgrace. More silence.

"My suggestion to you, Miss Richards, is that you take advantage of what you have. Date the fine men who ask you out. Get involved with the religious activities on campus. Attend to your studies."

Whew, that sounded like a reprieve. Wait a minute. He made it seem as if he knew I'd refused every returned missionary who even wanted to have a lemonade with me. How would he know? I gathered up my books to leave but he kept me glued to my chair with his stern expression. He pressed his lips together looking at the ceiling for so long, I couldn't help but look up, too.

"Just before you came in," he said in a soft voice, "I'd been going over another student's background. He did remarkably well on his entrance exam. He's applied himself. I don't know how he's had time to learn so much. His life hasn't been easy. He reads Greek and Latin plus speaks three other languages."

The dean stopped, looked at me as if he expected a comment. Why would he tell me about this guy?

The phone rang. The Dean turned away to answer.

I reached over, picked up the student's folder. It read "Harold Styler." I checked out his picture. Well, nice looking in a too serious way. His mouth looked pursed, prudish almost. I looked over his class schedule. Then I saw the note on the right hand corner: "non-Mormon." That interested me. How many could there be on campus? The Dean finished his call. I handed him Harold Styler's folder. Did he want me to look him up? There had to be some point in his telling me.

"These files are confidential, Miss Richards." His tone matter of fact. He didn't seem surprised that I had looked at the folder.

He gave me a curt nod. I figured it meant I should leave.

Now what? I was intrigued by this non-Mormon guy. What harm could there be in checking him out?

# Chapter Twenty-Three

I waited outside Harold's classroom. No trouble spotting him, Harold stood taller than most of the students. I gave him a big smile as he walked by. He ignored me.

Next I followed him to the cafeteria, took a seat beside him.

"Hi, my name's Karlan. And I know your name is Harold and you're not a Mormon."

He looked at me for a full minute. I forced my eyes to stay with him even though part of me wanted to forget the whole thing and get out of there.

"You want to convert me?" he asked finally.

"Just the opposite. I want to spend time with someone who doesn't have an agenda . . . for me, I mean. My family is devote Mormon. That's what the Dean called them. I'm not. I don't have anything in common with the returned missionaries."

We sat in silence. I tried to think of something else to say. Then it came to me. "There's a Sadie Hawkins dance coming up. Would you be willing to go with me?" I smiled at him. He glanced quickly at me then looked away. Guess that meant, no. I concentrated on getting out of my seat as gracefully as possible.

"Are you always this forward?"

I stopped halfway out of my chair. "This is a girl ask boy deal. That's the way it works."

"But we don't know each other." He paused between each word.

"Sort of the point, right? To get to know each other. Can you dance?"

A small pause. "Yes, yes, I enjoy dancing." Finally, he smiled. Nothing generous, just a slight lilt at the corners of his mouth. What a difference it made. His deep blue eyes took on warmth. His mouth became sensuous. He had a perfectly symmetrical face. I paid attention to how faces fit together. Mine looked like someone in a big hurry had slapped two halves in place but—missed by a fraction. I sat back down. He kept looking at me.

"Karlan, interesting name. Where did it come from?"

I felt the tape begin to run in my mind. I relaxed spieling out one of my familiar stories.

"My father's name is Karl. The doctors told my mother, 'no more babies after this one.' So I got my father's name. But no one can tell my mother what she can do or not do. Two brothers followed. Name got wasted on a mere girl." My voice took on the sadness of fate. I had more to say but Harold held up his hand like a policeman stopping traffic.

"Sounds like you've told that story a lot. Do you believe it . . . the part about being 'wasted on a mere girl?'"

No one had ever asked me that. For a moment I wasn't sure.

"No, not really." He sure knew how to deflate a good story.

"That's what I thought. Yes, sure, I'd like to go out with you. Why not? I haven't danced for a long time." He looked wistful. "What dorm are you in?"

"Do you want me to write it down for you . . . . with the date and all?"

"I can remember," he told me firmly. "What dorm are you in?"

I found my heart fluttering. That hadn't happened since I arrived on campus. Come to think of it, it hadn't happened since, since when? Since I foolishly thought myself Bob Andrew's top priority.

# *Chapter Twenty-Four*

Harold brought a bottle of handmade carrot juice instead of flowers. I accepted his gift but couldn't think what to say.

"We could have some now," he suggested.

"Ahh, no thanks. We just finished dinner."

My five roommates stood around us in the kitchen. After meeting Harold they didn't disperse like planned. Maybe the carrot juice held them captive. Ann took the bottle.

"We'll have it for breakfast," she said cheerfully. Ann then handed it to Ruthie who passed it to on to Gay. With great ceremony, Gay put it in the refrigerator. I thought of the game "hot potato."

As Harold and I made our departure, Ann held me back. She whispered in my ear, "Long night ahead, Dynamo."

I didn't know what to expect but I felt awkward. When we stepped onto the dance floor everything shifted. The stiff, formal guy I walked in with changed into a fluid, elegant dancer. Music must be the key. I started enjoying myself when he maneuvered to the side and stopped cold.

"You're leading. I don't want to struggle with you. The man's supposed to lead, okay?"

"Okay."

My hands began sweating. I had a problem with that. He didn't pull me tight to his body but close enough so we moved as one. I began to feel graceful. I smiled at other couples. I even daydreamed that girls envied me.

The drive home turned into something different. "Sooo, Harold, why did you come to the BYU?"

Silence. He went back to being stiff, kind of strange. The dancing seemed like an aberration.

"Ahh, did that question seem too personal?" I meant that as a joke. He didn't laugh.

Finally he looked over at me. "No. Of course not. I'm just thinking what to say. How to explain."

Good grief, what could there be to explain? "It's so complicated?" I started to feel worried.

"I'm picking up a few psych courses," he mumbled and looked out the window. "I have the credits to graduate now." When he turned toward me, he looked worried, nervous. "I'm a lot older than you are—seven years."

He made it sound as if the campus police would be knocking on our window any moment.

"Big deal. We're both college students." This guy took himself seriously. "Am I understanding you right? You came to this university to take psych courses?"

"No, no, not just for that. I wanted to study—the Mormon religion."

What little enthusiasm I had left, whooshed out of me. A student of religion. Good grief. He might as well be a returned missionary. Now I didn't know what to say.

"My special interest is nutrition." He looked as if I should be impressed. "Mormons see their bodies as a tabernacle to be protected. That attracts me."

Oh Lord, the guy sounded like a prissy old woman. Get him off that subject in a hurry.

"Ah, Harold, tell me about your childhood, your family."

I watched his face close down. He looked sour, old enough to be my father. All I could think about was getting back to my normal roommates.

But come to think of it, I wasn't exactly normal. I made a good show of being "just like them." I wanted to fit in. I hadn't said a thing to my roommates about not being a believer or my other struggles. I did tell Ann and Ruthie my reading difficulties but that didn't put me into a weirdo box.

I looked over at Harold. He seemed uncomfortable but not as up tight as before. What did I have to lose? I hadn't talked to anyone about what went on with me. We'd never see each other after tonight. Why not just let go?

"Okay. You want to be quiet? I'll tell you about me. I've been labeled unteachable." I said that with a certain amount of pride. "Obviously that's an overstatement but I do have trouble reading, doing numbers and I get lost. Also . . . . also . . . . I have hallucinations on occasion and I see auras—lights around people. Otherwise, I'm just your ordinary freshman BYU girl."

He laughed. "Okay, you're an entertainer, Karlan. You already told me that but you shouldn't make fun of people's mental struggles."

"Harold, I'm not making it up. That's part of who I am. I'm a lot of other parts too. I'm telling you because we don't have anything in common. This night is, well, something like being inside a bubble. When it's over, it will be gone. I'm tired of pretending." I turned toward him, my voice heavy with tension. "I'm not interested in nutrition, nor in Mormonism. I wanted a light hearted date with a guy who, who wasn't all serious and earnest about stuff."

He looked over at me. He took his foot off the gas, letting the car drift slowly on the deserted street. The silence left me awash in peace for just one breath. Then he put on the brakes, pulled the car into an empty parking lot, killed the lights. My peace disappeared. I had a quick moment of fear. It vanished when I looked at his face. I saw interest. But most of all, I saw kindness.

"Tell me, Karlan, about, about your hallucinations."

# *Chapter Twenty-Five*

"Why are you being evaluated by a psychologist?" Mother's voice held panic. "What have you told people. You'll be, you'll be labeled."

I wanted to add, "and no man will marry you," but I didn't. "It's okay, mother. I talked to a neurologist. I had some headaches but they are gone now." The headache part was a lie but it calmed her down.

After a pause she asked the question that highlighted all her calls.

"Are you dating?"

"Sort of. I'm seeing a guy you'd like. He's smart, attractive."

"What's his name?"

"Harold Styler."

And then the question I knew she'd ask next.

"Where did he serve his mission?"

"No mission, mother. He's a student of religion and psychology. But nutrition's his main interest, at least at the moment. We don't have a thing in common. We just keep going out."

"Should we fly out to meet him? How serious is this?"

"We've been dating two months and he hasn't even held my hand. No, don't fly a thousand miles to meet a guy who is not attracted to me."

I didn't tell mother that I couldn't stop thinking about Harold. I looked forward even to studying with him, anything to share his space. He remained almost clinical with me. He gave me tests, even I.Q. evaluations, but didn't act personally involved.

I had seen a neurologist but not for headaches. Harold had set it up. At his urging I told the doctor about my hallucinations. We talked for more than an hour. Dr. Rayworth didn't seem concerned.

"When the brain can't process what's happening, hallucinations serve as a valve. Your brain developed this technique early. When you can remember why you needed that first hallucination, you can quiet your mind."

That made sense to me. But I didn't like his brushing off auras as something my mind made up—like hallucinations. I had been losing my ability to see them. I wanted my auras back. They gave me important information about people around me. I hadn't seen Harold's aura. He knew me. I didn't know him. The next day, as soon as I stepped out of the car, I took his sleeve and turned him toward me.

"Are you giving me all these tests to decide if I'm worthy of your time?" I could feel the heat rising in me.

"Of course not."

"Then why do you look uncomfortable."

"Okay, I am interested in what you can do. I want to figure out why you have trouble reading, whether your hallucinations have anything to do with it. Don't you feel better after talking to Dr. Rayworth?"

"Yes. Yes, I appreciate you getting him to see me."

We walked together without a word toward our destination. Harold and I had found a little hideaway among some trees. A few boulders, along with mossy grass, formed a small oasis of privacy. I sat on the ground with my arms wrapped around my knees. Harold sat on a flat rock, his legs stretched out in front of him. I had rehearsed what I wanted to say.

"Harold, I need to know more about you. You're a mystery man. If you don't feel comfortable enough to talk about yourself, I think we should stop seeing each other."

Whew! Big risk for me. I'd faced the truth. I was smitten with this guy. A week before, I had tried to get him to put his arms around me by deliberately stumbling. He did hold me for a second but spoiled it by saying, "Be more careful."

Now he looked off toward the trees. I waited.

"You've told me so much about yourself, Karlan, but you never mentioned—Bob Andrew."

"What? Where did Bob Andrew come from?" I felt off balance. "You know him?"

"I met Bob at a concert, when I first arrived here. We spent a lot of time together, less since I met you. We ran into each other on Monday. I told him I'd met an interesting, attractive girl. He wanted to know your name. When I said, 'Karlan Richards,' He stumbled backwards. It obviously shocked him."

My turn to sit in silence. At first I could only hear Harold's words, "an interesting, attractive girl." That's how Harold saw me? But Bob's reaction, almost brought me to tears. Did he think we still had a future? Bob hadn't called me when I arrived on campus. I expected the call. I waited for it. But then, I didn't call him either.

"I guess it seemed unlikely," I spoke slowly trying to make sense of it. "A coincidence for you two, well, I mean, so many students on campus . . . that you both should know me."

Harold sat very still. Not looking at me.

"Do you still have feelings for each other?"

"Of course, we dated all through high school. I care for Bob. I always will. But I'd only disappoint him. I realized, oh, a year ago, we had no future, I mean together."

"Did you ever talk to him about auras and hallucinations?"

"No."

"Why did you tell me?"

"I don't know."

Harold moved slowly toward me. His hand came across my shoulder, around my neck, up to my cheek. His fingers felt warm, strong. His breath smelled sweet. Gently he kissed me.

"Thank you, Karlan, for trusting me."

# *Chapter Twenty-Six*

"The night we met . . . that first night . . . ."

Harold stopped, as if he didn't know what he wanted to say. His voice sounded strange. We sat close to each other, parked on a side street. All afternoon the sky hung heavy. I wanted rain. I wanted something to happen. Now, at dusk, the clouds pulled together, tight, dark. The car had a cave-like feeling.

Weird day. Harold had no interest in seeing a movie, not even a free concert. The time dragged. I tried to be cheerful. I'd just received an "A" on a paper. Harold had helped me but it had been my work. I couldn't break into his bleak mood. I tried. I told stories about my roommates, my teachers. I even made up stories. But I couldn't make him smile. I turned toward him now, emptied my mind. He had my total attention. Finally he started talking again, not to me, to the windshield.

"You told me about fleeing Paris when the bombing started. Do you remember telling me about that?"

"Sure, I, I made conversation. You didn't want to talk."

"That's what I want to tell you. The 'why'. The reason I shut down, couldn't pull a word out. I couldn't even think straight. You told me about your nurse screaming, 'The Germans are coming. The Germans are coming.'"

"Yeah. I remember telling you that. I equated Germans with monsters. I saw hulking brutes in my dreams with big clubs beating my poor nurse to death. I'm over those nightmares now. So what about it?"

"I won't blame you if you want me to go away. I didn't think we'd keep seeing each other. At first, I only wanted to help you, not . . . ." He took a long breath. "I should have told you before, before I kissed you."

"What are you talking about?"

"A German *has* come. I'm the German."

Empty. I needed to say something, even a joke. When I looked at Harold's ashen face, I couldn't think of anything funny. His hands shook. I placed mine over his and waited.

"I'm not an American. I'm a German, born and raised. I came here at eighteen. Studied for a couple of years. Then went back to Germany. I, I worked as a translator at the Nuremberg trials. None of that's important. Not important. It's that . . . that I . . . I feel so ashamed of who I am."

I watched his face. I'd seen him tight before. But the tremor that held him now felt raw. I could tell he didn't want to be next to me. I could feel his misery.

"Don't pull away, Harold." I kept my voice calm. "Talk to me. What happened?"

"I should have told you. But that's been the problem. I'm a coward. I didn't want you to go away."

"I'm not going away. Tell me what happened."

He closed his eyes, held his mouth tight. The breath he finally took sounded ragged.

"I had a moment, a chance to make a difference, to be brave. To try, at least to stop one, one atrocity."

He wouldn't look at me. I hadn't seen tears falling but his face glistened wet. I couldn't grasp it. So Americanized. He even used slang. No accent.

Not any, no hint of his past. All this time, he hadn't trusted me. From the first, I had trusted him.

He broke the silence, his voice just a whisper. "I had a favorite teacher—good to me. He helped me. I'd always been afraid, deathly afraid of my father. I told you about that." Finally he looked over at me.

"This teacher treated me like a son. I saw the brown-shirts surrounding him. I heard him cry out, beg for help. I told myself, 'too many, too many. You can't stop them.' I ran away. I, I went back later, later, in the day. Only blood, only thing left of him, blood."

"How old were you?"

"Twelve. The same age as you when you were giving your graduation speech about the wind blowing. I know you. You wouldn't have let anyone hurt Miss Faucet."

I shook my head.

"Harold, we're all afraid of blind violence. If I were terrified, what would I do? I don't know."

I reached out taking both his hands.

"Right now, I can only listen. Harold, I'm numb. We've been seeing each other every day for more than six months. Now this. You've told me about your brother, your mother, stepmother, father, half sister. I thought I knew your family. I thought I knew you."

"Do you want me to leave?"

"Of course not. Don't be so, so dramatic. You accuse me of that." A quick surge of anger came, disappeared. Harold's face took focus again. I put my hand on his wet cheek. "You've taken my breath away, that's all. I have to blink, figure out my feelings."

We sat crowded in the Renault, needing space. Both staring blankly. The wind howled, giving the little car a shake. Finally a soft rain began to fall. I wanted to walk—alone—but I didn't want to leave Harold.

I'd felt at a disadvantage with him. He did everything well, knew about the world. I stumbled along trying not to sound like an uneducated ninny. I'd fallen in love. He told me he cherished our friendship. Hell! My heart had ached with the space between us.

Now everything changed. Harold didn't like himself. I thought about Joan wanting a machine to give her a new body. Harold wanted a new history. He wanted to be a whole different person. With all my problems, I didn't want to be someone else. Did I love myself? Yeah, I did. I liked me, even my confused mind, the way I saw stories everywhere. The way I enjoyed stranger's faces, reading them, thinking about them. I groused about my parents but I didn't want a different family. Could I help Harold? I didn't know. I stretched out my legs as far as I could in the cramped car.

One thing, Harold lost his mystic. A broken man wanted my acceptance. He needed my strengths, not the other way around. I didn't know if I could help him but I knew, almost instantly, I wanted to try.

# *Chapter Twenty-Seven*

"You can understand our confusion, Karlan. We send you to The Brigham Young University and, and you find a Harold Styler? How is that possible?"

Harold had captivated my parents. His understanding of Mormonism, his worldliness, his obvious intelligence on top of good looks, left them in awe. Harold's German background didn't phase them a bit.

"How did you ever pull this off? He's no one we'd expect you to attract. He's sophisticated."

"I guess, mother, my nurse had it right. She used to call me her little witch. I did it all with magic."

Mother shook her head. "We're happy for you, of course, but he knows so much more than you. Might that be a problem after, after the attraction wears off?"

"Are you worried I might bore him, mother? I don't think that's going to happen. I may drive him crazy, though." I enjoyed this encounter. I stood straighter in front of my mother than I ever had before. "Another thing, I doubt he's any smarter than Bob Andrew. Harold's simply older. He's had more life experiences. Bob never found me boring, either, by the way."

I didn't tell her about Harold's controlling nature or his scarred past. I didn't tell her that I worried about his inability to play. I didn't mention my mothering need to protect him.

After Harold told me about his past, we had two months of intense courtship. I never fell asleep in Harold's arms like I had with Bob. I wanted more intimacy, kept guiding his hands. I didn't care about the consequences but he wouldn't give in.

When he suggested a picnic dinner at our favorite hideaway and I saw he had a small bottle of champagne, my heart began a tap dance. Could he want a formal commitment?

"Karlan, I don't want to lose you," he took me by the shoulders. "The year's almost over." He sat down pulling me with him. He patted my hair, my cheek. "I have to make a choice, almost immediately. If I want to stay in this country, I have to join the military—to become a citizen. Otherwise, otherwise I have to go back to Germany."

The military! He'd never mentioned that before. Now I saw fear in his eyes, beads of sweat formed on his forehead. His words rushed at me.

"What do you think about getting married?"

"Married? When?" I moved away from him.

Harold got to his feet. "Don't sound so shocked. Where did you think this relationship would go? He looked hurt, defensive.

"It's sudden that's all. When are you . . . when would we . . . ."

"In six months. I'll have to go through basic training, then I'll get a leave. We could marry then. You, you could be a camp follower." He tried a small smile.

I had trouble breathing. I wanted this. But not now. It was all too sudden. We had problems, lots of problems. So much I didn't understand about him, about me. My mind swirled. I felt lightheaded, breathless. He kept looking at me. I had to say something. We knew each other's secrets. He never judged my strangeness. He seemed to honor it. I was safe with him. I wanted, I needed to uncover whatever haunted me. I could never do it alone. We both cared, deeply cared for each other.

Then the romance, the tender vulnerability, crashed and burned.

"Karlan, it doesn't have to be marriage for life." He said this as if to encourage me.

"What! You're asking me to marry you until . . . when? You find somebody better?"

"No! No, not at all. It's that people change. You may not want me in ten years. Maybe when you conquer your dragons, you won't need me any more."

"What about children? Don't you think that kind of arrangement is hard on them?"

"Yes. Yes, of course."

He looked like he hadn't considered children. He sat back down on his rock staring at me. "My father married three times. Each woman met his needs for different periods. It, it was always about him. It crushed my brother and me. I don't want to be like that." He sounded incredulous that I could suggest such a thing. "I don't know what I mean," he said finally. "I'm just so scared of making a mistake, for you as much as for me."

"Harold, look at me. I don't want to marry you as some kind of temporary convenience. I want a family, a commitment. Are you up to that?"

His face held such open tenderness, I didn't care what words he spoke. I knew his heart.

"You're part of me now," his words jumbled with sobs. "I couldn't live without you. I don't want to let you down. I, I'm afraid. I'm so afraid of hurting you."

I took his face in my hands. I felt a radiance sweep over me. Maybe this was what people called "a religious experience." Certainly, I'd not been here before.

"I love you, Harold Styler. I want to risk with you. Let's get married. January, January it is."

# Chapter Twenty-Eight

Five weeks before our wedding, I woke in the middle of the night with a storm rattling the shutters, whipping the curtains. Nothing for it but to close the window. A chair left in the middle of the room ambushed me. Tripping, I landed on my face, swallowed my front tooth, broke my nose, split my chin. Shock paralyzed me.

Mother came running in.

"Oh, no, no! I used your desk. You were so sound asleep. Then the phone rang. Oh God, look at you and your wedding's in a month!"

"Why?" I could barely talk.

"Ohhh, Karlan. I'm so silly. I started to think about our reading tea leaves. Remember? And, and Harold doesn't look like the man I kept seeing." Mother held a wash cloth to my face. "He was supposed to have dark wavy hair. Remember? Harold has dark-blond hair." Mother looked at me as if this made sense. "I came to your room to tell you not to worry about it. Just because he has blue eyes, doesn't mean he's not the right one. But you were sound asleep so I started to write a note. Then the phone—I forgot the chair."

I couldn't think of anything to say. What nonsense. I could never tell Harold what caused mother to leave a chair in my path. But, oh, how I needed to hear his voice.

Harold's words soothed me. "You'll heal. You still have your long blond hair. You can wear it like Veronica Lake—over your face."

That made me laugh which hurt.

"Ah, Karlan, will you have a tooth before the wedding?"

"Of course, it'll even be the permanent one."

Harold's leave gave us ten days together before the wedding. I couldn't have managed without him. He helped me prepare for my last two finals, catalogued all the incoming gifts, took mother on walks when she became tense.

The only spot Harold and I had for privacy was the guest room. I liked this quiet haven. The soft yellows and moss greens of the spread and curtains looked like an extension of the garden. The cream carpeting and walls soothed me. Mother had made an effort to have it special for Harold. A large potted red begonia sat on the French provincial table giving a dramatic accent. Two new satin chairs were at either end of the table facing the windows.

I slipped a note to Harold at breakfast. "Meet me at two—your room."

I lay waiting on the bed for his arrival. He smiled when he came in but didn't take the bait, choosing a chair instead.

"Okay, Karlan, you said you had questions—about my past. Now's your chance. I'll tell you anything you want."

"Don't sound so serious. Come cuddle me first, then we'll talk."

"Other way around. Sit over here."

"We'll do it your way." No point in quibbling with him. He'd been evasive for months. Finally, some answers. "Remember, Harold, when I told you about seeing auras? You asked if I ever talked to the dead. What in the world was that about?"

He got up, paced, sighed.

"Oh, damn, everything else is so much easier, dealing with your parents, all the work to get ready. I don't want to shock you." He looked at me. "Give me a moment."

Harold faced the windows. His arms rigid at his side, fists clenched. I got nervous. Maybe this wasn't a good time. Maybe, maybe I should put this off.

"Look at all those plants," I said cheerfully. "Father works on his garden every chance he gets even in the winter. I'm like him, you know, a farmer, a peasant at heart. You're not marrying an aristocrat, that's for sure."

Harold laughed. "No, let's get this over with. I'll start at the beginning. My mother's father, my grandfather, was a famous German medium."

He looked at me as if he had just announced that his family kept slaves.

"Okay, that's interesting. Go on." Why should that make him uncomfortable? I found it rather intriguing. Colorful ancestors added spice to our genes.

He watched me. Finally, in a calmer voice he went on. "People came from all over Europe. He, my grandfather, that is, believed he could communicate with special spirits sent to this earth to help us, us mortals."

"Ahhh, did that make Mormonism seem more plausible, familiar to you?"

"I don't know." He looked confused as if I'd introduced something out of left field.

He sat down, took my hands. The warm rush of trust we often had together washed over me. He lost his tense, ashamed look.

"I've felt so negative about this, this part of my past, so muddled. Maybe I've ignored the obvious. Could I be attracted to what I abhor?"

"Why should you abhor it?"

"Because my mother followed in his footsteps. She idolized her father, saw him far superior to my father. He must have known. My father forbade her to do this 'occult devil worship stuff' as he called it."

When Harold stopped talking, he held his lips tight to his teeth as he had when we first met. He took another deep breath. Then he looked at me and laughed.

"You have just shredded your mother's gorgeous begonia. Didn't you realize it?"

"No, I don't know why. I guess I felt upset for you. Gosh, what'll I do? Harold, tell mother you did it. She won't say a word." I listened to myself and shook my head. I sounded fifteen, still afraid of mother. "Forget the blasted begonia. Go on."

His smile faded. He closed his eyes, sighed again. "Mutti went behind his back, had her own devoted following. When my father found out, he gave her the choice: give this up or lose your children. She went off in defiance, I guess, to another seance."

"What happened? He couldn't take her children away from her."

"Oh, yes he could. You forget the times. Hitler didn't like mediums either. My father hated Hitler but would use him if it suited."

I wrapped my legs together like a pretzel, something I did when nervous. I couldn't think of anything soothing to say.

"He already had my stepmother in the wings. All I knew, at the age of seven, my mother disappeared and I couldn't even mention her name."

"Did you, did you ever see her again?"

"Yes, my brother and I found out what happened through the servants who sided with Mutti. We managed to see her. We'd get caught, punished. My father insisted he did it to protect us from, unhealthy . . . well, you know."

"No wonder you have trouble trusting. Only seven. Oh, Harold, I'm so sorry and then the war came. You didn't get many breaks as a kid. I understand better. It's clearer to me. You threw yourself into study. I guess, well, you needed to trust something."

Harold's eyes closed again. He leaned back in the chair, a sort of peace came over him. A peace that let his tears fall.

# Chapter Twenty-Nine

I spotted my wedding dress through the window of a small boutique. It had leaves in muted green falling through wispy fog. It had a flowing skirt. So what if it didn't look like conventional marriage attire. Trees were my talisman. Between classes at Wayne State University, I rushed in, bought the lone gown—a size too big.

"We'll need two weeks to alter this," the seamstress said around the pins in her mouth.

"I don't have two weeks, just ten days."

"Why would you wait so long?" She scowled at me.

"Never mind. Can you do it?"

My parents had bought Harold a handsome suit. I dreamed of him waiting for me at the bottom of the stairs. I planned to dazzle him as I gracefully descended.

I clutched my list of "must do before the wedding." I never let it out of my sight. Fifteen items had been scratched away. Number sixteen, "Wedding Dress," done. I gave a sigh of relief. Two items to go. It looked like I would make it happen, after all.

Twenty-four hours before Uncle George would pronounce us man and wife, I sat waiting for the hair stylist to make my best feature glamorous.

"Trim the ends and set it, please," I told her. "Forgive me if I sleep. I just finished my last exam. I'm so tired I can't think." I took the time to pencil out, "exam," number seventeen, as well as number eighteen, "hair." I crumpled my finished list, tossed it the trash and with a happy sigh, fell asleep.

I woke to find my hair cut off to what the beautician called an attractive "bob."

"This is much more flattering," she told me. "You have a small head. All that hair accentuates the problem. Makes your face just about disappear. You'll love it by tomorrow."

"Did my mother tell you to do this?" My voice sounded flat. I'd become paranoid after the chair incident. But my mother had nothing to do with it. When she came to pick me up, she screamed. She said she'd sue. I had trouble calming her. We left without paying.

When Harold saw me, he stumbled for words. "Is that legal, to cut off your hair without permission?"

"Probably not. But what can I do? If I had told her I was getting married tomorrow she wouldn't have done it. I fell asleep. Guess it's my fault." Harold shook his head, looked resigned. Finally he hugged me.

"Well, let's see. You still have your good figure. Try not to do anything to that between now and tomorrow."

Father picked up my dress the afternoon before the wedding. A late night meeting kept him in town until well after I had fallen asleep.

The next morning my college roommate, Ann, shook me awake.

"Get up. This is your big day. You get the bathroom first. I'll help you." She looked at me carefully.

"You know what? I kind of like your hair. It is attractive. And your bruises have faded to the point of artful makeup—you know, accentuating your cheekbones. You look sexy."

I didn't when I put on my dress. It hadn't been altered. Joan grabbed a needle and thread making big basting stitches. Ann pulled the back together with a diaper-sized safety pin. Only a half inch of silver showed along my backbone.

"Just face the guests at all times. No one will notice," Joan assured me.

I held myself straight as I walked down the sweeping stairs to Harold. His eyes got big when he saw me. He bit his cheek to keep from laughing. I had managed to make my figure look like I "had" to get married.

Only the immediate family, plus three close friends including Miss Faucet, came for the ceremony. I had invited Miss Painter but since she didn't get along with mother, she declined. Two large receptions followed to accommodate all my parent's friends—business and church.

Over and again, I explained to the guests that Harold and I would live in Manhattan, Kansas.

"Oh, dear," said one woman whom I had never seen before, "what a dreadful place to start a marriage."

"No, it isn't glamorous," I agreed. "But Harold might have been sent where I couldn't join him. This way, I can finish college." My cheeks hurt from smiling.

"We'll have a proper honeymoon when I'm done with the military," Harold told another inquisitive women.

He managed to be charming through the long afternoon. He kept his hand on the small of my back hiding the safety pin. With my arms tight to my side down to my elbows, I covered the stitches. Perhaps no one noticed my dress. Perhaps I looked just like I had dreamed.

When the last guest left, we gathered our belongings to leave. But mother started crying.

"What's the matter?" I asked with a feeling of dread.

"You're too young. I need one more night with you in your bedroom. Please, my heart can't take the pain."

She clutched her chest.

"Is this something in the Mormon tradition?" Harold whispered.

I shook my head. Mother did look sick. I didn't know what to do. Giving into her would mean losing our honeymoon night at a romantic country inn just an hour away. My Aunt Ruth gave it to us as a wedding present. I had dreamed of it through the hectic weeks. I would have Harold alone in my arms, to start our lives together in a charming, romantic setting, to finally have sex. Oh, the joy of it.

I tried to reason with mother but her tension increased. Her whole body shook. At first she flushed, her breathing rapid but then she turned ashen, leaned into the wall. My father looked bewildered. No help from him. No matter what I did, I'd upset someone. I might do real damage to my mother.

"Okay, we'll stay one more night." I said it with finality.

Harold looked at me in disbelief.

"I'm sorry, Harold. I'm so very disappointed. I wanted . . . . I needed . . . . Oh, hell. I'm going to bed." I reached for his hand. He brushed it aside, said nothing, turned toward our guest room.

# Chapter Thirty

The knock came before dawn. I slipped out of bed, cracked the door. Harold's stern face greeted me.

"Let's get out of here."

"Right," I answered. "Everything's ready."

Once free of the house, he exploded.

"What a hell of a way to start a marriage. Why do you let your mother control you?"

"Wait a minute. You always defend her, telling me I don't understand her sensitive nature." I shook Harold's arm. "And you were there too, by the way. Why didn't you say something?"

"I'm not going to carry you out of your parent's home." He stared straight ahead then let out a whoosh of air. "I do admire your mother, in many ways. But last night, last night, she totally manipulated you." Finally he looked at me. "Once you said we'd stay, she suddenly got well." Harold shook his head. "Did you see how she swept up the stairs dismissing all of us, like, like some kind of queen?"

"Yeah, I saw her miraculous recovery. Why would she do it? I mean having us stay one more night. What could she . . . . ?"

"I have no idea."

The sky darkened. Soft flakes drifted down. I wanted to embrace them. Fresh snow seemed like a new beginning. I smiled at Harold wanting to share the feeling. Then the wind picked up. Hail hit our little car so hard it felt like a scolding by the sky.

"Do you want me to drive for a while?"

"You've got to be kidding. I don't have a death wish, at least not yet."

"I'm not a such a bad driver."

"You don't pay attention to the conditions. You drive too fast, too close to the car in front of you. You have no idea where your wheels are. Aside from that, you're great."

"This is a lot of fun."

Harold looked over at me. His face softened.

"Now look who's letting your mother control the situation and she isn't even here. I'm sorry. Let's start the day again."

I scrunched down in the seat letting good feelings replace the upset.

"Did you know about the punch bowl mixup?" I asked.

"Something else went wrong?

"I'll say. The champagne and vodka mix went to the Mormon crowd by mistake. Of course, they were supposed to get the fruit punch with seven-up. Dad couldn't let some of them leave until they sobered up. Kind of hard to explain."

Harold actually laughed. He finally looked relaxed.

"That's quite a story. I understand your parents being worldly enough to want champagne for their daughter's wedding."

"Well, Joan didn't have any at her wedding, nor did Hal. Of course, they married in the Salt Lake Temple."

"I don't hear longing in your voice, do I?" He smiled over at me.

"Good heavens, no."

We drove in silence for a couple of hours.

"When do you want to stop? Get something to eat," I asked.

"Didn't you pack food from the kitchen? Those leftovers could feed us for days."

"No, I came right away just like you asked." The good feeling started to melt.

Another hour passed.

"Harold, I have money. When we were in the reception line, women I didn't even know kissed and hugged me while slipping bills into the top of my dress. You know how it gapped in front? Maybe they felt sorry for me."

Harold gave me a soft look. "Maybe."

"They were business and social friends of my parents—not the church people. They must have heard we were struggling students."

"That sounds strange but I'm not complaining. How much money?"

"Five hundred and eighty dollars." I gave him a big smile, glad for a piece of good news.

"That's a godsend. I don't know what to pay first. We have your tuition, books, rent. I've saved what I could, but . . . ."

The conditions became more dangerous. Harold drove slowly. We watched for a motel to wait out the storm.

"Look, Harold, there's a good place to stay."

"And it would cost half a month's rent. Reduce your expectations, Karlan. We have to be careful for years."

"But, but we just got married. This is an exception, a special occasion." My voice came out a whisper. I felt small, the fight gone from me.

Harold found a little grocery store. I let him pick out the food: cheese, crackers, a bag of nuts, two apples. I didn't argue. I had no appetite. A heaviness pulled me down into a fog-like limbo. I hadn't known this place before. We drove another twenty minutes in silence. The wipers struggled, pushing snow mixed with hail. I felt the weight, the weariness of trying one more time and then one more time.

A dingy motel blinked through the sleet. The vacancy sign brought us to our "honeymoon spot."

Yuck! The moment I stepped in the door, my nose rebelled. I came emotionally awake. Someone had been sick or something had died. All the disinfectant cleaner couldn't erase the odor. The bathroom appeared worse. The tub probably had been cleaned but with the rust stains, I couldn't tell. Harold stretched out on the bed in exhaustion. I didn't say anything, crawled under the covers with my clothes on.

# *Chapter Thirty-One*

Sometime in the early morning, Harold pulled me to him. He caressed me tenderly.

"Karlan, I'm nervous as hell. I'm just as inexperienced as you. I've read everything I could find, but firsthand, I know nothing." He half sat up, supporting himself with one arm, head resting on his palm. "I want to make this good for you. This place is all wrong. Sometimes I'm such an idiot. I wish I'd stopped where you wanted." He bit his lip, looking like a wayward child. "Should we wait for a better setting? We could take another day, go someplace elegant. What do you say?"

"Nooo, hold me. Make love to me. Let's start now with our marriage and forget the last two days. I have enough imagination to turn this dump into paradise." I kissed him hard. What he'd said about being an idiot, wanting to make it right, the woebegone look. All of it, unleashed what I'd felt before, before our dreadful wedding.

"Listen," I cooed dreamily, "you can hear the ocean lapping on our beach, our private beach. Moonlight is creeping over our thick cream carpet. Satin sheets, feel them. What color? Ah, deep green. And flowers, big bouquets. Harold, let yourself smell them."

Two hours later we lay bathed in sweat, both miserable. He threw his arms over his head.

"My God, if it's this hard, how could there be overpopulation? I, I'm hurting you."

"Please Harold, just do it. I read it, it might . . . . It's expected to hurt."

"I might damage you."

Who was sobbing? Me? Harold? My face felt sticky with tears, mucus. I pulled the skin on my abdomen, twisting it.

"I can't stand it." The first words came out a scream, then died into a mumble. "I'm not made right." I wasn't talking to Harold but to something out there, apart from either of us. "First my mind—now this. Something's horribly wrong. I'm all wrong."

I stumbled to the rust-stained tub longing for a scalding bath. I wanted my body to feel alive again. The water came out tepid. I sat in it anyway. After a while I looked up to see Harold at the door. He didn't say a word. He had the motel's frayed sheet over his shoulder. He put out his hands to me, pulled me from the tub, wrapped me in the sheet. He carried me back to bed, held me in his arms, rocked me.

"This is what I think. You have a thicker hymen than most women. That's all. You're not made wrong." He kept rubbing my back, stroking my short hair. We'll have it checked out tomorrow. No, today. It's five o'clock, Karlan. It's the beginning of a new day. It's going to be okay. The good news is, I know a gynecologist."

I tried to follow his words. My mind seemed to slip into another place with a strange whirring screech. Harold took my face in his hands.

"Listen to me. It is going to be fine. I'll make an appointment in the morning. We'll go straight there."

"What are you talking about?" I looked around the room. I couldn't understand what I was doing naked with sheets all over the place.

Harold stepped back. He stayed very still. When he spoke his voice sounded faraway. "Didn't you hear what I just said? Karlan, concentrate. I know a doctor. I went to his house to buy a used hi-fi. I just told you that." He spoke clearly as if talking to an accident victim. "I got to know Dr. Erckman. I trust him. Born in Germany, trained here." Harold's voice went in and out, the screeching sound kept invading. "We talked a long time."

"Who did you talk to a long time?" I touched Harold with a finger to make sure he was real.

"The doctor. The gynecologist. I told him about you. He's the one to see."

"But that will cost. You said we don't have any extra money. Why not use the military. Isn't it free?"

"That's better, Karlan. Now you sound like yourself. And it's a good question. Yes, the military is free, but I trust this doctor. You never know who you'll get when you go to the army clinic. I'm not an officer. And, there's no privacy in the military."

I felt like a child. I didn't question kind Dr. Erckman or what he did to me. I don't remember any pain. Years later Harold told me I had a short stay in the hospital. I have no memory of it. When we finally consummated our marriage, I felt numb. Through it all, Harold remained loving, supportive.

"Give it time," he said.

# *Chapter Thirty-Two*

We had a tiny apartment fashioned from a former laundry room. The basement windows let through muted light. Huge old wash tubs served as storage for our clothes. We shared the moist dwelling with legions of the biggest cockroaches I'd ever seen. They crawled up through the wide drain in the middle of the cement floor. Nothing we put over it could keep them out. I didn't care. Harold treated me with tenderness. I became passive, grateful, estranged from my body.

When he told me of his plan to help me read, he acted like a partner not a teacher.

"I have no idea if this will work. It's a stab in the dark. What I want to do is form new neurological pathways in your brain by teaching you through touch."

"You mean I'm going to learn braille?"

"No, not at all. You'll use the same Roman letters but learn them a new way."

He had made the alphabet into sandpaper letters that fit the width of my finger.

"What an enormous amount of work you've done. You did all this before the wedding?"

"Yes." He sounded embarrassed.

It seemed a tedious chore. I tried to envision him bent over his bunk, alone at the army base, making letters—to help me. I felt breathless. I kept seeing a different person, someone complex and fragile. Someone with hidden strengths yet with rage that made him frightening. Right now, helping me, he was the most gentle of men.

We sat together on an old blue-velvet love seat he'd found at Goodwill. Classical music played in the background. I wore a blindfold. Harold guided my finger over the letters, telling me the names. We repeated the exercise over and over. Images flowed from my finger to my brain. In the darkness of my mind, the letters swam with colors, darting in all directions, jumbled and chaotic. Harold formed the letters into simple words. Again I would feel them through my fingers allowing my mind to see a picture of a "toe" as well as the individual letters that spelled the word. He rearranged the letters to form a different word, then another. Simple sentences followed: "The cat sat. The blue vase broke," etceteras.

"What we're doing, Karlan, is starting from scratch. I want to get rid of your old way of seeing words with reversed letters. Maybe now you can start to read without panic."

"That sounds good."

And it felt good, snuggled next to Harold, sensing his patience. It took months but the words gradually became benign. The chaos lifted.

During one of our sessions, Bach's Toccata & Fugue in D Minor began to play. My mind seemed to explode, letters and words shredding into flames. I tore off my blindfold.

"Stop! I can't stand it. Turn off the music."

"It's Bach, Karlan. You, you love Bach. What happened?"

"I don't know. I don't know. Everything turned red. I saw, no I guess . . . more like I felt . . . little, just for a second. I think, I might have been standing under a table. What was I trying to do? Light a candles, that was it."

"Keep trying to see. Look around you. Where are you?"

"A church, huge. There's a smell, I know but don't know. Candles. I can't reach them. I have to do something. The organ's playing. Dread. I'm in dread. And I can't get away."

Harold rocked me as he had on our wedding night.

"God, I don't own my mind. A sound can undo me. I'm sure I've heard that Bach Fugue before but with the blindfold, everything changed."

"I don't want to push you but if you can remember, anything at all, tell me."

"I don't want to think about it. Let's leave the blindfold for now. Maybe if you read to me like Miss Faucet did, it might be safer."

Harold agreed but seemed disappointed, maybe frustrated. He spent so much time reassuring me, I couldn't figure out how he truly felt. I flowed in pleasure with his quiet reading. He relaxed, giving way to a new direction.

Shakespeare's most famous plays came first, then Goethe's *Faust* and on and on. After we read for a half hour or so, we'd talk about it. I liked that part best. Harold never made me feel my take on the material inferior to his. My mind raced back and forth, pulling nuances together, forming my own ideas. Harold looked surprised by my interpretations.

"I don't see it that way. But there isn't a right or wrong way to interpret literature. That's what makes it so, so rich. Anyway, there's a whole world of ideas waiting for you."

I continued with my classes at Kansas State University. I actually became an "A" student, except in math. Harold requested a stay for the duration of his tour so I could finish college. The army responded by transferring him immediately to Munich, Germany.

# Chapter Thirty-Three

Harold sat with his head in his hands. "I can't go back, not in an American uniform." He crunched deep into the chair, his fists clinched. "Not until Germany heals—until I heal." He spoke the last words in a whisper.

"What's the worst thing that could happen, Harold? Imagine that, then figure how to avoid it."

He didn't look at me, kept shaking his head. "It's, it's that I feel powerless. The army can do what they want with me. Like in Germany, I'm helpless. I had to wear their uniform, had to carry a gun. I never had any say about anything."

He had only three weeks to anguish before being shipped to his motherland. The whole time he spent in misery. Our home seemed to close in around us. I couldn't find a way to help him. He wouldn't let me in. I felt imprisoned but not with him. I was an outsider, caught—unprepared.

Finally the day came for him to leave. Relief, massive relief. After all he'd done for me, I could hardly wait for him to be gone. My desire to push him out the door produced guilt and shame but it didn't override my joy in the freedom about to be mine.

Another two weeks of classes, then exams meant I could be alone in our little cellar. It made me giddy with pleasure. I ate chocolate all day long, steak for dinner, sweet rolls for breakfast, all forbidden foods. I wandered the streets at night, feeling safe in the college town. I went to movies Harold would call romantic fluff. I did absolutely what I wanted. Why not stay all summer? I could get a job, study German, earn money for my ticket. I could stay longer, maybe until Christmas. I could have another semester of school.

One night, walking in moonlight, a feeling of rapture rushed over me. I missed Harold. I missed him with an ache that made everything seem dull—even the taste of chocolate. It surprised me, thrilled me.

"Find us a home," I wrote him. "I'll figure out how to pay for my passage."

His return letter had money. It read like the man I knew. "I found a place, a huge room in an old mansion. The best part, we can afford it."

What a sweet reunion. Harold's patience in lovemaking had long since paid off. When I stepped from the ship, I saw a tall man with half the flowers of a florist shop in his arms. I moved out of his way, searching the crowd for Harold.

"Karlan," the man whispered.

"My god, Harold. Is that you?"

I crushed him in a hug while he tried to protect his bouquet. "What in the world! I've never seen such flowers."

"I asked for a riot of color." He beamed at me. "The florist insisted I learn the name of each one. Remember our wedding night? You made up bouquets to fill our drab room." Harold talked like an excited teenager while still clutching me. "I forgot most the kinds you said but I did get the roses. See this rose? It's rare. It's called 'Angel Face.' It has the best aroma. These are Iceland Poppies, great color but they don't smell. The ones in the middle are Alstroemeria ligtu. I bet you didn't know that name. Aren't they dramatic? Over at the corner are more poppies but they're called 'Shirley', and Iris, of course. You called Iris elegant, remember?" He stopped, suddenly self-conscious. A crowd had gathered. Amused faces caused us both to blush. I with joy.

Harold brought me to an intimate inn for a long weekend. My flowers dominated the small but charming room. "Hang the expense," he laughed. "You're here."

Next, he took me to our new home. The stone house looked impressive with massive trees surrounding it. The wrought iron fence gave it a look of grandeur.

But our landladies, two grouchy, pinch-faced old women, were less than welcoming.

"You share the bathroom with three other families. Be quick. Always clean the sink and toilet after use."

Their contempt for Americans came with every word. My dying bouquet felt like my spirits, wilting with each new discovery. Our cold dark room felt like a cave. The dingy ornate ceiling sneered at us. Mustard colored drapes looked heavy enough to crush us. I tried to be cheerful but already I missed the cockroaches.

# *Chapter Thirty-Four*

"How should I greet your father? Should I embrace him or . . . . ?"

"No, no, be . . . a . . . be subdued. He'll probably kiss your hand—formally. He'll stand at attention, give a slight bow at the waist. Let him make all the moves. Expect both my father and stepmother to be distant but polite."

I'd seen two pictures of Harold's father. One, as a twenty-year-old student. Even at that tender age, he looked forbidding with a strong profile, no smile, hard jaw. The other picture, from a newspaper, showed him as the powerful director of a large steel mill. He stared at the camera defiantly. His driver stood at attention holding the door of his black automobile.

"Is that a Mercedes, Harold? It looks impressive."

"Well, made by Mercedes, but this car was a Mayback Zeppelin DS 8. At the time of this article, everything began changing. He sold or lost the car, gave it all up."

The picture showed so much. Harold's father looked to pause before entering his automobile, as if granting a special favor to the photographer. His face was that of a man used to giving orders, being obeyed. The article said he would retire at the height of his career but gave no reason. Harold told me the decision came because he didn't want to work for Hitler's war machine.

"Why didn't he get into trouble?"

"Because he didn't openly defy the Fuhrer. Father did it carefully. But powerful people knew what he'd done. He's principled, always has been. But, but a harsh parent." Harold looked melancholy, uncomfortable. He had told me about having his knuckles rapped at the dinner table for picking up the wrong fork, being thrashed with a cane if he didn't instantly mind. I shivered, took Harold's hand.

"One thing I have to remember," he went on, "when there wasn't enough food near the end of the war, he fed Manfred and me first. Neither my stepmother or father made a show of going without for our sakes. I don't know what else to tell you, Karlan. Be yourself. He won't eat you, I promise."

"What about your stepmother, Hedi?"

"I have no idea how she'll react. Prepare for anything. She's volatile. You have to expect that from a concert pianist."

"Does she still perform?"

"Oh, no. My father would never allow competition. She gave up her career, her friends, everything for him. Her Steinway dominates the living room but she doesn't play it anymore."

I knew Harold's signs of distress: biting his lip, hunching his shoulders, dropping his head. He showed all his body-language-misery while describing his family.

"Did I tell you Hedi tried to teach me piano? I hated having to sit next to her." Harold walked slowly through the sodden leaves, in no hurry to arrive at his father's home. "I guess I never gave her a chance. She replaced my mother so I . . . Karlan, all she ever got from me were sour looks and defiance. I know she didn't tell my father or I would have been punished." He looked at me. "Why couldn't I have been grateful for that?"

We rang the bell of the ground level apartment. It had been Herr Stieler's large home but he had divided it into four units with the loss of his wealth. Harold had "Americanized" his name to "Styler." I didn't know how this might sit with his father so I carefully practiced the correct pronunciation. "Herr Richard Stieler, Herr Richard Stieler."

The door opened quickly. A tall woman with wild hair stood before me. Her large face broke into an enormous smile. She glowed from within. "Karlan? Karlan, you're here, at last." She grabbed my hand. "I've waited for you half my life. Come in, come in."

As I stepped through the threshold, she wrapped me in her arms, hugging me with such strength, I gasped.

"Let her breath!" said a firm voice. Harold's father took over the room. He dominated the thick carpets, the heavy paintings, the rich brocades, the dark—hued furniture. His shaved head seemed massive. Harold looked shriveled beside him. Hedi noticed, placed a hand on Harold's arm. I saw him relax—slightly. All this took only seconds. I started to put out my hand to Herr Stieler but he pulled me to him, held me gently, almost as if I were a wounded refugee. I felt a surge of warmth. His smile could only be described as tender. Instantly, I had been adopted.

# Chapter Thirty-Five

"Come, come," said Hedi. "See the feast I've made for you?"

And what a feast, cheeses, roast beef, half a ham gussied up like it wanted to steal the show. Couldn't do it though. The floral centerpiece had it beat. The flowers looked like Harold's bouquet, the same riot of color. There were platters of fruit, salads, pickled herring, rolls, breads, tiny sandwiches—all of it made my head spin. Hedi had covered the buffet table with plates of pastries. Champagne bottles sat proudly in buckets of ice. The bounty felt welcoming, almost overwhelming.

"This is a grand party," I said in awe. "I'm, I'm amazed at such a lavish . . . How many are coming? You must have worked for days."

"More like weeks. And the only person besides you and Harold will be Manfred."

"Manfred will be here?" Harold whole demeanor changed with the news.

"I get to meet your brother, too." I gave Harold a hug. "This is a celebration."

I had thought a good deal about Manfred after seeing his sad-looking photograph. He stood on a train platform saying goodbye to Harold who was leaving for the United States. The two feared their separation permanent, so grim were the times.

Hedi broke into my thoughts. She gently touched my arm realizing I had gone elsewhere. "Did you know Manfred just completed his Ph.D. in engineering? With his new job, we didn't think he could come. But when he learned Harold had brought his bride, well, no one could stop him." Both Richard and Hedi spoke English with strong accents but I had no trouble understanding them.

Manfred didn't look like the sad picture from seven years before. He had filled out. He had become self-assured.

When Harold introduced us, we just looked at each other smiling, not touching. It felt comfortable. Manfred nodded his head as if something became clear to him. Then he pulled me into his arms.

For the rest of the afternoon, we feasted. Hedi beamed—almost shy with our appreciation. Later she and I took a long walk. In no time, we became friends. Hedi shared her life on the stage. She told me about her frustrations in wanting to be part of Harold's life.

"He's a very good tennis player, you know. I so wanted to cheer for him at tournaments but he forbade me to come." Hedi shook her head.

"That's mean," I turned toward her. "Shame on Harold."

"Actually, I understood but still, I hoped for a breakthrough. Now, I have you." She grabbed me around the shoulder, pulled me into her. "It is now all better."

When we got back, I sat alone with Richard and Manfred. Harold had taken his father's car to replace a worn tire. Hedi insisted in doing the dishes by herself.

"I'll get you next time. This first visit is to give honor—no work."

I sat with the men in smiling silence until Manfred cleared his throat.

"What will you do with yourself, Karlan?" He asked this with kind eyes.

"I, well, I want to learn German. I'm feeling, what, inadequate. I'm not good with languages."

"Maybe you could find a position in an English speaking business. Learn German slowly, comfortably."

That hadn't occurred to me. "What a good idea, Manfred. Wait until I tell Harold. I'll let you know what happens. I mean if I find an establishment that will hire me."

Harold helped me with the want adds. No one seemed to be looking for a non-German speaking woman of nineteen with few clerical skills. I found three that were nonspecific enough to give me hope.

I was able to report to Manfred that the first place I tried, Radio Free Europe, hired me on the spot. I had a great job culling news as it came over the wires, being an office gopher and even giving tours to visiting dignitaries. I made more money than Harold. I wrote Manfred about my boss, Mr. Conners.

"He's head of the whole thing." I told him. "I confessed I didn't type well plus I had difficulty spelling in any language. Mr. Conners only laughed. He said his seven-year-old son had trouble reading. After I told him how Harold had helped me, he said he wanted me in the executive office.

"I don't care if you can't spell," Mr. Conners said, 'if you've overcome seeing letters backwards, you can figure out anything around here."

I didn't tell Manfred the next thing I asked of my new boss, nor did I fully explain my strange request to Mr. Conners. I felt anxious, but even more, I felt desperate. I had had an hallucination in the middle of the night in our horrid, new home. Harold thought it a continuation of a nightmare. I knew better. I squared my shoulders, looked directly into Mr. Conner's eyes. "Could I come in late—two days a week? I know it seems a lot to ask." I bit my lip. "I want to do psychotherapy. A colonel—he's a psychiatrist. He's agreed to take me on."

Mr. Conners paused only a moment. "Yes, but let's keep this to ourselves."

# Chapter Thirty-Six

"Psychoanalysis is no picnic. Is this something you want to go through?"

Damn, Dr. Clements looked stern. He wouldn't be any picnic, that's for sure. His stiffness blocked out good looks. His haircut, too close to his scalp, made him look like a teenager with wrinkles. Boy, did I feel nervous. It didn't help that his face showed no emotion. I took in a big gulp of air.

"I'm here because I want to figure out why I see things that aren't . . . that other people don't see. I want to understand why I go into panic when I hear a certain piece of music. I want to know who I am. I don't expect a picnic, Dr. Clements. And I haven't been on one."

He didn't look as cold as when I first came in. Still no animation but more thoughtful. He turned a pencil over and over in his fingers, letting it bump on the desk. It bothered me. I didn't say anything. I wanted to trust him. I so wanted to trust this grim-faced colonel with all the right credentials but not an ounce of warmth.

"Have you ever seen a therapist before?"

"When I was fifteen, I stayed with my older sister, Joan, in Provo." I took a deep breath, clutched the arms of my chair. "I had two intense hallucinations close together. Of course I didn't tell Joan. She would have fainted. But it scared me. So I lied about my age, gave a phony name. I talked to this psychiatrist in Salt Lake. I told him about the hallucinations. He wanted to hospitalize me on the spot. I . . . I said I had to use the restroom. Then I ran like hell."

Colonel Clements raised his eyebrows a fraction but said nothing.

"I saw a neurologist in Provo. He, the neurologist, said my brain made hallucinations to relieve pressure when . . . I got upset. He told me something happened early that I couldn't handle so I started this bad habit."

"Did he use the word, 'bad?'"

"No. No he didn't but . . . ."

"What do you think is going on?"

"If I knew I wouldn't be here."

My anger surprised me but not Colonel Clements. His eyes sharpened, then he smiled—slightly.

"When you're having an hallucination, do you ever think it's real?"

"Heavens no. I'm always aware it's my brain but still . . . ."

"Do you hear voices telling you to do things."

"Nooo, nothing like that. I'm not crazy. At least I don't see myself that way."

This wasn't going the way I hoped. I wanted Dr. Clements to tell me lots of people had hallucinations but kept them quiet like I had. "Nothing to worry about," I wanted him to say. It didn't look like that would happen. Okay. Okay, tell him. Tell him everything. I licked my lips, looked right into his eyes. "I hear different sounds, echoing, muffled. Sometimes I hear conversations as if behind closed doors. This happens when I'm all alone, no one to hear for real. Usually there's a . . . . a whirring noise, like machinery. But it's the special smell that . . . ."

"A smell?"

"Like burning garbage. I can't think how better to describe it but it's very distinctive. When the smell comes, I'm stuck. The images follow. Usually . . . . a huge hand coming at me."

He closed his eyes, leaned back in his chair. After a long pause, he quietly spoke. His face had softened. "Do you understand Harold's fear about my writing anything down?"

"I . . . I didn't know he . . . My mother feels that way. She's afraid of what might be done to me. Maybe she's afraid of the stain on our family. I'm, I'm not sure."

"Your mother received shock therapy?"

That surprised me. How would he know? Of course, Harold had told him everything he could about me, about my family.

"Two different times," I finally said. "But I don't know how many treatments. It left her distrustful of any kind of doctor."

"A fear like that is powerful," Clements said. "It can spill over on to children. Are you afraid of doctors?"

"Psychiatrists scare the hell out of me."

He almost laughed, at least his eyes crinkled and a sort of "humph" sound jumped out. "Harold's fear," Dr. Clements went on, "stems from what happened in Germany during the war. Anyone who had mental challenges might be carted away—as a drain on society. Did he tell you about seeing his elderly neighbor forcibly removed from his house?"

"No, he probably didn't want me to . . . . What was wrong with the neighbor?"

"Dementia, I'd guess."

"You're telling me that Harold's afraid someone in our government could do me harm if . . . . ?"

"Your job at Radio Free Europe would be in jeopardy." Colonel Clements said it softly but it had the heaviness of truth.

"Oh."

"Harold wants you to receive help but not be labeled. He has a point about 'no confidentiality' in the military. So, I'm not making many notes.

FROM THE CLIFFS OF PYLA

I'm leaving things out. He put the pencil down. Looked at me for several seconds.

"You can trust me, Karlan."

Right then, I liked his hazel eyes.

# *Chapter Thirty-Seven*

After that first day, we met in a little room adjacent to his office. I stretched out on a leather chaise lounge looking at the ceiling. Dr. Clements sat behind me. I only saw his face at the beginning and the end of our fifty minutes.

"What's on your mind?" he asked after I settled on the couch for our first session.

"Harold wants me to bleach my hair."

"And that's the big thing bothering you?"

"Well, we fought all weekend. You see Harold everyday. You should get a pretty good idea about our lives. Are you treating him too?"

"Absolutely not. Harold's seeing a German psychiatrist. Your husband works under me. I supervise him. I don't treat him."

I started to twist my head to look at him. Stopped. Dr. Clements waited for me to settle again.

"I won't tell Harold about our sessions—ever. You'll be discussed with the other four therapists in our clinic." He stopped.

Maybe I should say something. I didn't know what he wanted from me, what the rules were.

"Also," Clements went on in a quiet voice, "I see the same German psychiatrist Harold sees. There may be a time when I will discuss you with him. In a way, Dr. Brennberg will be treating both you and Harold. But you're my patient. You understand that, right?"

"No, I didn't know any of that. Not until just now." Feeling queasy, I put my hands on my stomach. "I, I feel anxious, sick almost." I said it to the ceiling. "The idea of people I don't know talking about me."

"I'd be surprised if it didn't bother you." Silence.

Finally, Clements spoke. "Tell me what upsets you about changing the color of your hair."

My tension disappeared. I could deal with this. "See, I don't want to be made over—turned into someone I'm not. I hate the idea of putting poison on my scalp. Harold feels cheated because my hair is turning dark." I started talking fast. "Harold likes the Nordic look. It used to be sun-bleached—my hair, I mean." I pulled at it, wiggled my toes feeling restless, like in school. I waited, waited. Why didn't Dr. Clements say something? I needed clues. I needed to see his face, understand how he felt about . . . . I searched for something to say.

"Did Harold tell you how he helped me read? Now I read all the time. It's just, well, he . . . . Now he wants me to read in German. He says novels are pap. I'm not stretching my mind." I looked up at the white popcorn ceiling. It made me edgy—too much white. I could hear his clock tick, ticking.

"I mentioned bleaching my hair to my boss, Mr. Conners. I wanted him to say I look fine as I am. But he told me, he told me, 'That's a good idea. I think you'd look better, more attractive, as a blond.' It made me sad. Much sadder than I would have thought."

"I can hardly hear you," Col. Clements said in a loud voice. "I need to hear what you're saying."

I wanted the hour over. I felt like, like a turtle stuck on my back. The silence made me feel anxious, like I wasn't holding up my side of things.

Finally Clements spoke. "Harold tells me you're taking ballet to be more graceful. Whose idea is that?"

"Harold's, of course. All the other students are kids and much better than I am. When it's time to go, I feel more awkward than when I came."

"Why don't you quit."

"Fights not worth it."

"What about your hair?"

"I'll bleach it. I'll let the beautician tell me how to wear makeup. I'll get new clothes. I guess how I look is part of my job. I want to please Mr. Conners. It's just . . . there's so much in my head to work on. I want the outside of me to be okay. Something, anyway to be okay."

"Do you always give in so easily?"

I started crying. I worried about the collar of my blouse getting wet. My eyes would be red-rimmed. I had to go back to the office. I had to . . . to look good.

# *Chapter Thirty-Eight*

My nightmares got worse. Dr. Clements told me it meant progress.

"Can I have a pill that lets me sleep without dreaming? I mean so I won't fall into this scary stuff. Just one night a week."

He didn't answer me. I waited, like always, feeling the quiet prick around my eyes, like a rash.

Finally his voice came, reconnecting me.

"Anything different about last night's dream?"

"Not too different, nasty, big monster-man, like always."

"The monster still sleeping?"

"Yeah, and still has that stupid look."

"Why does that scare you?"

"See, I can't reason with something like a shark. Something with a . . . a what's it called? Reptilian brain. He's going to kill me if he wakes up. In the dream I know that for sure so I have to be . . . careful. Like, my life depends on it." I wanted to turn around, look at Clements. Maybe he sat back there with a big smile on his face, thinking me ridiculous or something. I kept my eyes on the ceiling. One of these days, I'd turn around.

"Go on," Clements sounded firm.

"Last night he was sleeping just like always, snoring, and I'm walking around trying hard not to wake him up. But, you . . . you were there for the first time standing in the door looking at him, not me. You were careless." I said it with anger. "You let the door slam."

"And what happened?" Clements actually sounded interested. Real emotion, for goodness sake.

"I don't know what happened. I woke up in a sweat and never got back to sleep."

"After you got over being afraid, did a thought or memory come to you?"

"Yeah, weird. I remembered my father coming to my room after midnight—to rub my back. Nothing life threatening in that."

"What did you do about your father coming to your room?"

"Well, first, I stopped sleeping in my room. I hid all over the house and then I took care of the problem by getting married quick as I could." I felt out of breath but hadn't moved a muscle. "So can I have medication for sleep? I need a break"

"No."

"Just no, without a reason?"

"You don't need medication. Your mind does a fine job of letting you remember just what you can handle. Trust your good brain. It's protected you all these years."

"You think so? It seems to me it's caused all the trouble."

"You're alive to the world, Karlan. You're doing fine."

After that session, I practically skipped to work. "I'm doing fine. I'm alive to the world."

# Chapter Thirty-Nine

Dr. Clements shocked me, took my breath way.

"Why stay in a relationship that makes you miserable?" he asked at the end of a session. "You have choices."

"You're telling me to leave Harold?"

"I'm not telling you to do anything. I'm saying . . . you . . . have . . . choices."

I took an hour walking to my office at Radio Free Europe. I sat in my chair ignoring the stacks of work in front of me. Mr. Conners walked to my desk, looked at me, walked away. He came back an hour later. I still sat doing nothing.

"I guess you didn't have a good session?"

I looked up at him but didn't answer. I stayed late, finished up.

Sometimes sessions swept by so quickly, Clements's clock would "bling" almost as soon as I stretched out. At least it seemed that way. I left his office with headaches that lasted hours, dizziness that kept me from typing or reading. Pieces of memory slipped out unbeckoned. Clements connected parts here and there with questions that rattled me.

"Did you find Harold's damaged spirit attractive?"

I didn't know what to say.

I'd leave his office feeling I'd run a marathon.

Some days neither Dr. Clements nor I said much of anything. I put Kleenexes on my face like blankets, letting them fill up. I longed to hear the clock's chime giving me freedom, at least for a few days.

I dragged off to work, wondering the point of it all.

It was at this time, Harold decided to reenlist. We had talked about it for months. Since he didn't have a graduate degree, he felt his training under Dr. Clements the best he could receive. His own therapy had been moving rapidly. A German psychiatrist better understood Harold's painful history.

Near the end of one session with Dr. Clements, I turned around. I needed to see his eyes. It didn't startle him. He raised his eyebrows in question, waiting.

"It's been a long time since I had an hallucination. Even my nightmares are tame. Maybe I'm finished. Maybe I'm well. Maybe you cured me."

"Do you believe that?"

I didn't answer. I sat slumped looking at my feet.

"No," I finally said.

"I don't think so either," he told me in a gentle voice. "I'm glad Harold has reenlisted for your sake as well as his."

I walked slowly to work. My mind a muddle. I had tried so hard to dig out my deepest memories but I kept tripping over my relationship with Harold. Harold, who wanted me free of my demons, became one of them. He longed to see me soar, wished me to dazzle. I felt buried by his hopes, his projects for me. Peace, that's what I wanted. I fought him for my right to be ordinary. But I'd give in, try to do who he wanted, try to please him. Where had the gentle man gone? I liked who I had discovered when we lived in Manhattan, Kansas.

I started running, not knowing where. I didn't know who I wanted to be with. I didn't know if I even wanted to be with myself.

I let my bleached hair blow wild and kept running.

# *Chapter Forty*

I met Mutti, Harold's mother, the first week we arrived in Germany. She had a radiant face with gray hair in a braided bun. Strands of pure white broke free. It looked like a halo. Her luminous blue eyes showed no age. She gave me only kindness, but still, I had an urge to flee whenever we were alone together.

We had been in Germany two years when my impacted wisdom teeth needed extraction. The army liked efficiency so all four got pulled at once. Within a day, my face ballooned. A high fever confirmed infection.

"No point in your waiting for hours in the emergency room," Harold told me. "What can they do but give you antibiotics? You stay in bed. I'll pick up the medicine."

No argument from me. I felt like hell.

"Harold, wait," I called out. "Don't forget to lock our door." Despite my sore face, I smiled at the memory of Herr Tonkin, one of the other renters. He had stumbled into our room in the middle of the night searching for the bathroom. Poor old guy believed himself in the home of his youth. We thought we'd been attacked by the boogyman.

I heard Harold lock the door. I went right to sleep. It seemed like only a moment before I woke to the sensation that someone stood near me. I tried to make out a face in the darkness. It looked like Mutti. But she couldn't get through a locked door. Whoever it was, began stroking me, murmuring in German. Am I so ill I'm being prayed over? Nothing made sense. The room seemed to be filled with fog. Everything moved in a slow circle. I heard chanting. God, I'm sick, really sick. Where's Harold? What's happening?

The door flew open. A light blinded me. Was that Harold? Yes. He filled the whole doorway. He gave a piercing yell.

"Yoouuuu!" He elongated it so it became a curse.

His words sprang like swords, thrashing the air. He spoke German. I couldn't understand all of it. He said something about poison . . . about her poisoning me. How could she poison me? She only stroked me. Nothing felt real but the terror inside me. What did I fear? Not Mutti. No, not Mutti . . . Harold. His face looked ugly. A table crashed. Had he thrown it? I don't know this man.

"Harold, what's happening to you? Your mother isn't doing anything to me." My voice came out a squeak. I couldn't get through to him. He grabbed her shoulders. "Don't. She's fragile." I had to stop him. Get out of bed. Move, move. Then, nothing. It all went black.

When I woke, Dr. Clements sat on the edge of my bed studying me. An open doctor's bag lay at his side. I put my hand on the bag to make sure it was real.

"How you doing?" he asked me as if we'd run into each other at a picnic.

"Strange, really strange," I whispered. "What happened?"

"You got up too fast, passed out, cracked your noggin on the metal bed frame." He checked his watch. "You've been in and out for the last forty-minutes. But I think the main reason you're confused is you have a fever of 105. Plays tricks on your mind."

"What happened to Mutti?" I could hear the panic in my voice. My God, had Harold killed her? His face looked terrible enough. I searched the room, no Mutti, even on the floor, no Mutti. Harold. Where's Harold?

Okay, I see him now. Sitting way off in the corner. Such a dark, gloomy room.

"I put her in a cab, sent her home." Dr. Clements had a casual drawl when he wanted to downplay something.

"She's fine," he went on. "You're the only casualty." His voice held a soft melody I hadn't heard before. "By the way, did you give her a key?"

"No, of course not."

"I took this away from her." He held a key about six inches from my face. "Do you recognize it? Harold said you only have two keys."

"Mine's in my purse. It doesn't look like that. I don't know where it came from."

"Remember," Dr. Clements asked, "when I told you that you are my patient, not Harold? Right this minute, that isn't the case. I need to . . . to help Harold. You need to sleep. Harold's going to wake you every couple of hours. I'll see you first thing in the morning. We'll get x-rays but I don't think you need them. You'll be fine . . . so will Harold."

I watched Colonel Clements take my husband's arm, lead him from our room. That stranger over there, that man I had never seen before, was my husband.

# Chapter Forty-One

Harold had two emergency sessions with his psychiatrist, Dr. Brennberg. All the fury had left him when he finally talked to me. His voice sounded flat.

"She wants you, you know? Thinks you have a special mind that can flow between the two worlds. She told me. She thought it would please me." He gave a cry that sounded like a wounded bird. "When I saw you lying there so helpless, with her hovering over you, I exploded."

I sat absolutely still, hardly breathing. Dr. Clements told me I had nothing to fear from Harold but still he seemed an alien. I listened carefully, wanting to understand what had happened to him. He looked drained. After taking a deep breath, he went on in the same dead voice.

"When I turned fifteen, I finally got permission to visit my mother. I couldn't see the truth even then. I dreamed of the moment we'd be together without fear of my father. I thought she'd be excited to be with me." He got up, began pacing. More energy came into his voice. "When I saw her with you, I knew. She hadn't wanted a son. She wanted a follower, a disciple. Now she wants my wife." He said the last part with his teeth-clenched. It startled me, I pushed back into my chair. Dr. Clements had warned me not to block Harold from saying whatever came.

"Give him comfort," he told me. "Try not to get pulled into his drama. Right now he needs to be little and you need to be the adult."

I went to Harold, put my arms around him. He felt pliable, letting me put his head on my lap. I wished he wouldn't talk any more. It felt like his heart might leak right out of him. I held onto what Clements had said. I didn't stop the flow. I couldn't mend him. But I could hold him. He pulled his legs into a fetal position, fell asleep. A half-hour later, when he woke up he went on as if no time had passed.

"All these years, I blamed my father," his voice was quiet again, "for separating me from my beloved mother. I thought she longed for me . . . but she, she didn't care enough to give up her seances."

The next week Harold seemed more himself.

"There's something I need to tell you, Karlan. I've talked it all through with my psychiatrist."

We were sitting together for Sunday breakfast. I had put a vase of flowers on the table wanting to break the grimness in our ugly room. Classical music played. I had squeezed fresh orange juice, made omelets in the landladies' kitchen. With still warm rolls from the local bakery, our little meal felt nurturing.

Harold pushed the mushroom omelet around on his plate, tore open a roll, ate nothing. Finally he started talking again.

"I understand something about why I keep trying to change you."

Now he had my total attention. I forced myself to lean back, keep my expression calm.

"It excited me at first. You, you were . . . so different," he stammered. "I remember when you told me about seeing auras. It made my heart beat fast." He began stacking dishes as if he didn't know what to do with his hands. "All of the unusual parts of you attracted me. Because, because my mother had seemed so mysterious, so wonderfully different. She saw things I couldn't see, just like you." He stopped, took a long breath. "Then, then it . . . it scared me. I had to make you someone else. Someone I could trust." Harold looked flushed. He sat on the edge of his chair. I stayed still, remembering Clements's words. Harold didn't seem to expect me to say anything. He pursed his lips. I had hated that look. I didn't know why it bothered me but now I saw it differently. He needed to hold himself together. I could see so much more being quiet, watching. Harold took my hand. "I keep waiting for you to tell me your going to leave me," he finally said. "I seem to do everything I can to make that happen. But . . . but it's the last thing I want."

# Chapter Forty-Two

I put shredded paper in an old pie tin, added twigs, put my diaphragm on top then lit a match. I watched the mess burn. Well, it more smoked, sort of melted but I liked my little ceremony. Harold and I had been married more than three years. Colonel Clements told me I'd be a great mom. I kept repeating his words over and over, "You're going to be a great mom, You're going to be a great mom." When I told Harold, his face melted in wonderment.

"Oh," he said, "a child."

We had moved into a sunny, new apartment. Dr. Clements nudged, then pushed me to be assertive. Harold and I stopped lashing out at each other. Both of us learned to listen. Harold's psychiatrist also encouraged us to start a family. But it was Dr. Clements's faith in my wellness that mattered to me.

"You're not done with therapy," he told me. "You'll need to continue when you get back to the states. But I don't see any reason why you shouldn't have children since your marriage has become solid. Frankly, I'm surprised. I didn't give you two much of a chance in the beginning."

I became pregnant right away, ate only the most nourishing foods, exercised. I skipped to work, enjoying my job even more than before. I had no nausea. I felt powerful, all woman. Okay, I still needed therapy, but I

liked the strengths I found inside myself. No hallucinations, no nightmares.
I was going to have a baby.

In the middle of the third month, before dawn on a Monday morning,
I miscarried.

"I'm disappointed too," Harold said. "But this happens more often
than you think. It doesn't mean anything's wrong with you. We'll try again
in a little while."

That old feeling: "I'm not right inside," hung over me like a scourge. I
didn't want to wait for Dr. Clements's reassurance. He wouldn't be back in
his office until after lunch. I went to the clinic. I waited and waited to see an
obstetrician. Wives of enlisted soldiers couldn't be seen until every officer's
wife had been attended to, unless an emergency came in. Nurses must have
been in short supply. None attended the doctor while he examined me. I
tried to be light, make conversation.

"I guess lots of women lose babies in the first trimester? It's just that,
well, I've never been pregnant before. We were so excited."

The doctor stood impassive like a wooden Indian, arms at his side.

"Unfortunately," he told me while removing his rubber gloves, "you
won't be able to carry a child." He put the gloves in a shiny can. "Your
uterus never fully developed." He rocked back and forth on his feet. "It's
not quite infantile but it's too small to hold a baby—ever." He gave a curt
nod, left the room. I went numb.

I imagined Harold's face when I told him. He'd try to hide his pain,
try to support me. He'd tell me we could adopt. All the hollow words rose
like a boulder coming at me. I got dressed, walked out of the clinic, moved
without seeing. I felt a kind of dread, a guilt, a deep shame. My feet kept
going. I didn't have a plan.

Finally I ended up in front of Dr. Clements's office. I pushed the door
softly with my foot, waiting for him to look up. I didn't knock.

He stood quickly. "What's happened? I just saw Harold. He told me about the . . . but . . . wait, it's something else. Talk to me."

When I told him, he sat down with a thud, almost like he felt my shock.

"A gynecologist said that to you? He's a jackass. It's not true."

I wanted to hug him. Of course. It wasn't true. Jackasses got medical degrees all the time.

"But how do you know?" I started sobbing. "How do you know he's not a jackass who's right but insensitive and hateful."

"Because," Colonel Clements went back to his professional voice, "you've been seen by a far better specialist who performed surgery. He would have noticed an infantile uterus, for God's sake." Dr. Clements got up from his chair, stood in front of me. "The idiot you saw today . . . ." He sighed. "Let me tell Harold. I don't want him going off the deep end, punching a captain in the nose." Colonel Clements looked angrier than I felt. He actually stormed. I watched him, stared into his eyes. He looked away. Something . . . something wasn't being said.

# Chapter Forty-Three

"You need to see a physician you can trust," Dr. Clements told me the next morning. "I'm sending you to a female gynocologist who's 'on the economy.'"

I liked that. It meant she had nothing to do with the military. She wouldn't automatically make me a second class citizen because Harold was just a private first class.

And I liked Dr. Murcher. Probably Colonel Clements's age, her face showed more expression. She had dark-brown hair, skin that looked bathed in milk. She took time with me, answered my questions, reassured me.

"I have a colleague who is a plastic surgeon," she said. "She'll do a small surgery to help you secure a healthy pregnancy. You have some scar tissue."

"How did I get that? No one's said anything about scar tissue."

"No?" She stopped, seemed unsure how to go forward. "Call me Greta, will you please? What we need is a cup of tea."

It seemed so different from other medical appointments, I didn't know what to say. She heated water, brought out a tin of cookies all the time chatting with me as if we were old friends

"Can you think of anything that might have happened to you when you were very small? Anything that might have hurt you?"

"No. Oh, wait a minute, I did fall on my brother's bike—you know that bar down the middle? I was about six. It made me bleed a lot. Could that be it?"

"No." Then she looked closely at me. "Well, ah, who knows?" She drew out the words. "Yes, perhaps the bike. Don't worry about it. Keep seeing Dr. Clements."

I had the procedure. The plastic surgeon didn't give me tea and cookies but she made me feel safe, well cared for.

"You certainly don't have an infantile uterus," she said firmly. "Would you like me to give you a certificate so you could present it to that physician who upset you?"

"No thanks. I don't need to ever see him again." I smiled at her grateful for her compassion and anger on my behalf. "Just tell me when I can safely get pregnant again."

Harold and I waited. I kept on my health regime. I didn't need prodding. This body of mine would be so remarkable, our baby would never want to leave. As before, I became pregnant right away.

Four months later, I lost twin boys.

# *Chapter Forty-Four*

"What do you mean you're going to retire? You're too young." Dr. Clements had directed me to the chair in his office instead of his therapy room. "When will this happen? Not for a long time, surely not for months, not until we leave. Right?" I felt strangely betrayed.

"At the end of the month. I'll be gone in three weeks."

"Why? Why so sudden?" I wanted to grab him, tell him he belonged to me until I didn't need him anymore.

"My decision is personal. Nothing to do with any of my patients or my work as a psychiatrist." He looked tired.

"But I . . . . I feel so muddled right now." I searched his face looking for some opening. After my fourth pregnancy ended in failure, I thought he'd help me pick up the pieces. The only bright spot had been Harold. His kindness amazed me. No matter how angry or depressed I got, Harold stayed constant. Still, though, I needed Dr. Clements.

"I don't want you . . . ." What could I say to him? Nothing.

Dr. Clements left his seat behind the desk. He pulled a chair over, sitting so close our knees practically touched.

"Take a deep breath, Karlan. I need to talk turkey to you." He looked all business. "It's my replacement who concerns me. I've checked on him. You're the only patient I have who could be affected."

I searched his eyes. He looked serious, different. Clements went on, pulling me into his words.

"Dr. Cressland doesn't approve of prolonged therapy for an enlisted man's wife. I told you I wouldn't write things down but I've had to justify . . . such a lengthy process. When he reads your chart, he might want to do shock therapy. He's into that."

I jumped up. "But I won't allow it."

"Sit down. Let me finish. You signed a release to receive care from this department. He might try to force the issue. I don't want you to have a memory loss. You still have digging to do. You know that, don't you?"

I nodded. He stopped, letting his words hang in the air.

"Harold has just five more months," he went on. "I'll say your therapy has been completed. If Dr. Cressland should request you come in for his evaluation, You . . . don't . . . do . . . . it. You are on vacation. Quit your job. Stay low until it's time to leave Germany."

"I hear what you're saying, Dr. Clements." He was taking care of me the best he could. At least I could be appreciative. "Whatever has happened . . . that you have to leave so suddenly, I'm sorry. I mean for you. It doesn't feel like a good thing." I listened to the ticking clock. It should be in the other room. Everything had turned around.

"I feel bad about the way I acted . . . about your leaving, I mean. I only thought of myself." The sentence dangled. He didn't say anything more. He smiled warmly, stood up, stretched out his hand.

I never saw or heard from Dr. Clements again.

# *Chapter Forty-Five*

I dreaded our homecoming. No way could we avoid a confrontation about Mormonism. My belief in the interconnection of all energy would be anathema to my parents. How could I explain I hadn't been crazy when I flowed into a tree. I had been practicing my faith—in belonging to the universe. It didn't just exhilarate me, it healed me.

"I know what I'll tell them. I'll just say I'm still searching. Actually, I always will be so, it isn't a lie."

"It won't get better until you stop placating them." Harold said it kindly but I could hear emotional fatigue.

"I used to be a fighter," I told him, "a dragon. When I was a little bucked-tooth kid, no one pushed me around. Joan was sweet, gentle but I fought. And then . . . . I don't know. I changed. I wanted peace. I got addicted to people liking me. People like Bob Andrew, Miss Faucet."

"Then you got your fighting spirit back kicking me in the shins." Harold gave me a wry smile. "Don't think I didn't notice."

I grabbed my seat belt, feeling its resistance, wanting freedom, wishing our car wasn't heading for 9 1 1 Lone Pine Road.

"Harold, damn it, after all that therapy, I can't tell them how I think or feel without wanting to throw-up. This is so disappointing."

He reached over, putting a hand on my knee. He spoke in a tender voice that calmed me.

"Let's take a little time. We're early. I'll find a place to have a cup of tea. Maybe if you relax a bit, it won't seem so hard. Remember, we're partners. This is my decision too. You're parents can't possibly make you responsible for my beliefs."

"Yes, they can. After you got baptized, mother put the onus of building your faith on me. I didn't correct her. I should have told her years ago." I tugged angrily at the seat belt. "I didn't want a big fight before we left. And since then, in my letters, well, I avoided the subject. I wish you'd never gotten baptized."

Harold drummed the steering wheel.

"In therapy," he said, "I figured out why I agreed. I thought it was for your father so he'd feel good about our getting married. But the real reason, I wanted to belong to an extended family—where people brighten to see me."

We sat in a quiet booth nursing our tea. The red vinyl on the seat had cracked, been taped but still bit into my leg. It felt like a reminder. "You still need therapy. You're not quite whole, watch out, watch out."

"Okay, let's go fight the lions." I pushed up from the bench. "I'm as ready as I'll ever be."


Warm hugs were spread around. I felt my whole body flow to dear Mrs. Olson when she wrapped her full arms around me, pulling me into her huge, warm bosom. She'd been my parent's cook for twelve years. I didn't have to do anything to receive her love. Besides we had a long history of silent trust. Then my sweet baby brother threw himself at me, squealing with joy. The rush of warmth pushed everything else away.

Mrs. Olson served a vegetarian lasagna with her special savory tomato-basil sauce. The airy white cake with lemon filling, coconut frosting had been her idea. She glowed when presenting it.

Harold and I ate the luscious food slowly. Finally, I pushed back from the table.

"Oh, this dinner couldn't have been better. I love this beautiful house. I almost forgot how special it is. Thank you for the warm welcome."

My parents smiled. They had been beaming ever since Harold told them he had received a full scholarship from the University of Michigan to obtain his doctorate in psychology. The grant gave us enough money for the whole four years so I didn't need to work. I could go to school but, most important, I could try again to have a baby.

The mood was right. We seemed golden. Children to be proud of. How could they not accept our religious identity?

I carefully placed my folded napkin on my linen mat, cleared my throat.

"I'm not going to attend the Mormon church anymore." I'd finally said it but felt no relief. "I hate disappointing you. I have tried but I don't . . . believe."

No one spoke.

"You've both known that for a long time." My voice began to waiver. I could feel misery creeping up my back. "You keep thinking that if I just attend, it will eventually click for me."

Harold sat across the table. He watched my mother not me. When I grew quiet, he spoke up. "Please understand that I respect your belief system—for you." He looked first to my mother, then turned to my father. "I admire the strength of your faith. I know you both want what you think is best for us."

"You too, Harold?" Mother said it softly like the final blow had just been dealt.

Harold went on in a thoughtful voice, as if speaking to fragile people.

"I've studied Mormonism for years now. This isn't a decision we take lightly. I don't believe in the origins of the Mormon church." He put his hands on the table in a sort of supplication. "You know, I admire so many aspects of the Church. It' a fine organization but if I can't accept Joseph Smith's vision, I can't put my energy into it."

After my mother's brief comment, neither of my parents spoke. They got up and left.

Harold and I cleared the table, helped Mrs. Olson do the dishes. No one came to say goodbye.

# Chapter Forty-Six

A week later we received a summons for a family conference.

"We're in for it now, Harold. I think I'll be sick next Sunday."

"What can they do to us? Maybe the Tabernacle Choir will be in attendance. That would be nice. The Mormon church sure knows how to make beautiful music."

We didn't get the choir but my sister Joan, her husband, my brother Hal and his wife had all made a special trip, just to be a united force of persuasion. Everyone looked grim.

I gave out a happy shout when I saw Joan. "Hey, sweetie, what a great surprise."

She gave me a weak smile. Her hug intense but short. Her round, pretty face looked strained. I could see she had been crying. My twelve-year-old brother Bob sat on the floor in solemn gloom. Morgan was missing. I didn't know why. Everything seemed orchestrated. We were in attendance but not part of the program.

Father spoke without looking at us. "We're here to acknowledge that Karlan and Harold no longer want to be part of the Mormon religion nor do they want to keep their minds open to enlightenment."

I felt like saying something about believing my mind open but this wasn't my show.

Next we heard the testimony of each family member. I felt trapped, weary of fighting about ideas. I numbly listened, and listened. Harold studied each person with intensity. Could they be swaying him? Mother's breath came quickly. She closed her eyes. Perhaps she prayed. I felt a kind of dread. I seemed to lose years. I became younger and younger until I felt myself back in Paris with Mademoiselle Malmoray. She cajoled me, stroked me. I didn't want to be with her. Why? She had been my refuge. Long after we left France, I continued to conjure her up in my mind. I had reached out to her when overwhelmed. Now she felt like the enemy.

When I looked up, testimonies had ended. Everyone stared at me. Had I made some noise? I found my face covered in tears.

"Oh, Karlie," said Joan, "I can see how moved you are. You don't want to be separated from us."

"Of course I don't want to be separated from you. I just have a different religion. My tears are because I feel so uncomfortable with a family I love."

Father spoke again. He looked at everyone but Harold and me. I studied the wall of books behind him. This library had been a sanctuary for me when we first came. I used to pull out the huge picture books that always followed us from house to house. They were a connection for me. When I couldn't read, I learned about the world through photographs. Father had books about exotic countries. We seemed a house of the world, open to ideas and other cultures. Now the room seemed closed. I felt squashed. I wanted to find a tree, something alive and open to me.

Father's voice droned on.

"I know you understand that there are three kingdoms in heaven. Now that you have made the decision to leave the Church, you can not join the rest of the family in the Celestial Kingdom."

Joan began to cry. "I need you, Karlie, in my eternity. Please don't abandon me. Don't give up."

"Joan, for goodness sake, I'm not abandoning you by having my own beliefs."

On the spot, father called for a vote on whether we should be caste out of the family. On hearing this, Bob ran out of the room. Each one, even my beloved sister, Joan, and my dear brother, Hal, who had always been my protector, voted us out of the family. Without a word, my husband gave me his hand. I reached up to him. We walked out the door.

Bob, eyes brimming, raced after us. "You'll always be part of my family."

I reached down, hugged him. Something healing happened the moment our tears intermingled.

A mile down the road, Harold chided, "Gosh, I thought we might at least get dinner."

"You're trying to be funny. I've just been made an orphan. I feel . . . I don't know what I feel."

"That's because it isn't real."

"What are you saying? Do you think we're hallucinating?"

"Now who's making jokes. What I mean is, it won't stand. Can you imagine how this would play with your aunt and uncle?" Harold reached over lifting my seat belt to remind me I'd forgotten to latch it. I never forgot my seat belt.

"Lenore and George you mean?"

"Yeah, can you just hear it? 'Oh, we kicked them out of the family because they don't want to go to church anymore.' First of all, family is all important to Mormons. You don't cut your children out when they don't agree with you. Second, one of the most important tenants of the church is free agency. What they've done is total hypocrisy. Give them time."

"One thing Harold, did you notice that everyone bore their testimony but no one asked us what we believed?"

"Yes, I noticed. Something else, passed by them. We can't be set adrift. You and I are a family and they have no power to destroy that."

# Chapter Forty-Seven

Two days later mother called as if nothing had happened.

"It's Miss Painter," she said in exasperation. "There's to be a reception in her honor because she's finally retiring. I don't want to go. Your father would like you to serve as hostess."

Dear Miss Painter. I remembered stapling all her letters together the first time I came to her office. She only laughed. And now her retirement pulled me back into the family. Harold had said it would take about a week before my parents realized their maneuver had backfired.

"I would love to honor Miss Painter in any way I can," I told my mother. I didn't add that I wanted some time alone with father. I figured the thirty minute drive would give me enough space to say what I needed. I prepared hors d'ouvres and tea cakes for the reception. I wanted to give something of myself to Miss Painter.

When I got into the front seat, beside my father, it felt like an armed camp.

"You took me by surprise, dad. I thought you believed in free choice. You preach it then use 'shunning' as a control."

Father said nothing. His face looked stern. I watched the sun play on his auburn hair, wondering if I would ever again see his eyes full of love, laughing with me as we made up outrageous tales.

"Given our problem over the years, father, I find it hard to understand how you could throw me out of the family." My voice remained low but I could feel sweat drenching me. I started shaking. Father's head whipped around facing me. He looked shocked.

"What are you talking about, Karlan?"

"I'm talking about your night visits to my room.'"

"Nothing happened. I never did anything wrong."

"I so dreaded those visits, I stopped sleeping in my bed. I watched you from Morgan's room come to my door at two in the morning. What tore me apart was seeing mother watching you. She never said anything to me. You both had to know how miserable I was."

"I'd never do anything to hurt you." Father's voice broke. "I only wanted to rub your back, to let you know how special you are to me."

"And when you saw I didn't sleep in my bed anymore, it didn't occur to you that I didn't want your visits?" I watched his face crumble. I stayed quiet for several minutes. I wanted him to answer, to explain, but he didn't. Finally, I spoke again in a calm voice that surprised me. "Father, your back rubs at three in the morning were not what a daddy does to his teenage daughter."

"Where did you go every night?" He asked me as if I had been playing games all those years.

"Mostly I slept in Mrs. Olson's room, on the floor. I knew, for sure I knew, you wouldn't come to her room. Mother wouldn't protect me but Mrs. Olson . . . . at least with her I could sleep, be safe."

"Mrs. Olson, our cook?'" he sounded horrified. "She must have suspected something. What did she say?"

"We never spoke of it. Just as you and I never spoke of it. I don't know what she thought but she covered me with her blanket and gave me a pillow. I love Mrs.Olson."

Now I felt drained. I had worked on all this stuff about my father in therapy. Dr. Clements helped me understand that my instincts had been valid. The night visits held risk.

"Have you ever told anyone? I mean about your misconception?"

"Of course, I did, dad. I told Harold the first month after we met. It's one of the reasons I married so young. I didn't want to take a chance. And, I told my therapist."

"Did you tell Bob Andrew?"

"No, Bob thought—still thinks—you are the most outstanding man he's ever known. I wouldn't want to take anything away from his admiration. You are remarkable. You're known for your kindness, for your wisdom, but, in my case, you let me down."

I turned toward him, putting my hand on his arm. I wanted him to feel my presence while he rapidly denied what we both knew was true.

"I never felt angry with you. I blamed myself for being a temptation. I hated my body for diminishing you. This is only a tiny part of who you are but this 'one part' has caused me suffering. I should have talked to you about it. I didn't know how."

"I'm sorry, Karlan, you didn't think you could trust me. Nothing would ever have happened. I'm your father. I have always loved and protected you."

"You need to look at this, father, and forgive yourself."

"You told Harold? How can I face him. He won't understand."

"You don't know Harold. He doesn't judge. He even understands how desperate you must be to vote us out of the family."

# Chapter Forty-Eight

Father didn't benefit from having this wound opened, at least not that I could see, but I felt freedom. Finally I had spoken my heart and told him how it had been for me all these years. Also, the religious impasse felt less traumatic. My parents didn't notice my reduced tension. But I knew. Now I saw them more clearly. With Harold's help, I began to understand the pressures they had put on themselves.

I loved Ann Arbor. I just knew our first child would be born here. We had a charming apartment with an extra bedroom just waiting. I sat at the kitchen table, dreaming of our future when I heard the front door quietly open, silently close. Who had a key but Harold? I got up, alert.

"I can't do it, Karlan." Harold's voice sounded ominous.

"Can't do what? And why are you home in the middle of the day? Harold, are you sick?"

"Yeah, you could say that. I didn't go to class yesterday either. I just walked around."

"What's going on? You're scaring me."

He took me by the shoulders, his fingers dug into me. "I have to understand the body to understand the mind." I smelled tension on his breath, a sourness. "I need to go to medical school." He said the last part loud, like an order from someplace on high.

"Medical school! You never said anything about medical school." I pulled away from him. "Everything's been about . . . since we met you only talked about getting your degree in psychology." I kept backing away from him. "Harold, you don't mean you want to give up your four-year scholarship?"

"I already have. I've burned my bridges." He looked over at me, defiantly. "I don't even know if I'll be accepted to medical school." He sat down hard on a kitchen chair. "I'm too old and I'm missing premed courses." For a moment his head dropped. Then he got up, moved towards me. "But I'm giving myself no way out. It's either medicine or . . . or I quit school and get a job."

"How long have you . . . . ? You haven't talked to me. What happened to our partnership?" The enormity of it began to sink in. We lived separate lives. I tagged along while he dropped crumbs. "You son of a bitch, you didn't even consult me." I jumped up, slamming the pillow I'd been squeezing. "Everything's about you. I wanted this chance to get, to get my education while you got yours. To have a baby in a year or two. You've thrown my future away and never talked to me about it."

"If you don't want to support me in this, Karlan, then move on."

In that moment I hated him.

"Okay, I'm not helpless. At least we don't have kids. I'll 'move on.' By the way, it wasn't long ago when you told me I had a family—with you."

"Stop it, Karlan." His face looked gray. "I didn't say I wanted you to leave. I said . . . I said it wrong. I'm desperate. I didn't expect you to be happy but I thought if I explained why I had to do this, you'd be on my side."

"Well, I'm not. I just found out I'm alone in this marriage. You do whatever you want. You don't even discuss it with me. Then you tell me to get lost. You were a different person during our last years in Germany. We had a marriage then."

He stopped pacing, looked at me. He walked to the kitchen sink, splashed water on his face. When he came back to the living room he tried to take my hand but I pulled it away.

"I'm sorry, Karlan. I'm really, truly sorry. I should have talked to you. I knew you'd want to stop me. It's going to be such hard work—for both of us."

"You already counted me in, didn't you? Even before you told me, you had it figured out. Have you found me a job to pay for your tuition?"

"No, but yesterday, while I walked for hours through Ann Arbor trying to figure it out, I found a house."

"A house!"

"I know it sounds crazy." Harold's eyes darted all over the room.

"Our apartment is way too expensive but this house is cheap. We can fix it up, rent out the three garages."

"It has three garages?"

"It's old, maybe seventy-five years. The garages used to be a barn. And . . ."

"You're going to medical school and you want to buy a 75-year-old house?" Anger disappeared. I felt like Alice-in-Wonderland. "We've worked so hard for our savings, Harold." I was whining. I heard my voice but couldn't stop myself. "Now you want to use our hard earned money on a seventy-five-year-old house." Who was this fearful old woman inside my body? Harold didn't seem to notice.

"Okay, this is my plan. We fix up the house. We rent out the main bedroom plus the garages. That pays the mortgage, see. You work. We take out loans. At the end of medical school, we sell the much-improved-house and pay off our debts."

Somewhere during this explanation, he'd taken my hand. I hadn't noticed. Now he seemed to shrink. His shoulders slumped. His voice grew quiet. "That part is doable. The bad part," he massaged my hand to the point of pain, "the almost impossible part, I have to take premed classes that are filled and have already started. If the professors aren't willing to make an exception for me, I don't have a chance. So far no one's agreed . . . to anything. I went to the admission's office of the medical school, talked my face blue. I'm not given much hope. But . . . they didn't say, forget it."

"I need to know. Did you go to the medical school before you gave up your scholarship?" I pulled my hands away. Shook them, bringing feeling back into my fingers.

"After."

"I can't grasp this, Harold."

"Please help me, Karlan. I'll make it up to you. All of this: pulling the rug out from under you, not consulting you, putting off a child. I'll make it up. We'll have a good life. Help me now."

I felt numb.

"Say yes, say something, please."

"I don't know you."

"I don't know myself. I have to do this."

He stopped, licked his lips.

"You need to come. We have an appointment. The real estate agent has opened the house. I want to make a very low bid. If we can get this property, we can make it financially."

We drove to the other side of town. Neither of us spoke. The house, it's red paint pealing, sat on a quiet, tree-lined street.

"It's walking distance to the university. It's an original farm house before any of these other houses were built." He sounded like the real estate agent.

"It tilts. Is it safe?" I spoke quietly.

"I can fix the titling. I talked to a contractor. I'll put posts into the cellar and slowly crank them to even up the house. It's settled, that's all, but

I think its sound. The contractor's going to look over the house before we make a bid. What do you think?"

"It's hard to grasp." We walked through the front door. I noticed the wavy glass in the windows. "Are those original? They make odd slices of colored light. Like at a carnival."

"There you go. Now you're starting to see how unusual it is. And look at this stone fireplace."

"Yes, I like that too. It does give the house a solid feeling." I tried to imagine what fresh paint and deep cleaning might do. "I can see possibilities, Harold. The location's good. That's important." I looked at the floor and lost enthusiasm. The rug existed only where nails held it down. The exposed wood was old, rough and dirty. We climbed the stairs stepping over a loose one. It did have a banister. I liked the feel of it, as if someone had made it with a loving hand. Then I saw the bedroom door hanging by one hinge. "Harold, it's falling apart and . . . it . . . smells."

"That's mildew. We can get rid of it when we put on a new roof. The contractor . . . ."

"Harold, don't say another word."

# Chapter Forty-Nine

"Medicine's amazing." I heard Harold's voice before I saw him. "It makes me believe in God." He burst into our half-finished living room beaming. For the last eight months, his energy had been phenomenal. He completed the premed courses, entered medical school at the age of thirty, studied every night until two in the morning, worked on the house each weekend and still had strength to be excited.

"Karlan, wait until you see how intricate our bodies are. They work in perfect coordination; it boggles my mind. Will you just listen to this?" He walked in circles while thumbing through a foot-thick book. "Let me read this to you. You won't believe it."

I tried to look bright, even excited, but I couldn't grasp what made him almost froth at the mouth. I did make one lucky connection. "Hmm, this section sort of fits with what you read to me yesterday."

"That's it, that's it. You see the connection and it's only close, not obvious." He made it sound like a scientific breakthrough. "Karlan, you have to go to medical school. I love your mind. With your imagination, we'd be a perfect team."

I didn't answer. I felt too tired to point out the obvious. I didn't even have my bachelor's degree. Since I now worked full time plus two part-time jobs plus scraped paint off walls on the weekends, did the cooking, laundry, shopping . . . it didn't look too good for any kind of schooling in the near future.

The house did seem to be coming together. We had a waiting list for garage renters. The best room in our home, the master bedroom, had just been leased to another medical student. If only I weren't so tired.

Harold continued in a whirl of activity. He made jokes, kidded me about my fatigue.

Then came the crash. He slunk through the door late one Thursday afternoon, his shoulders bowed, his head low. He barely spoke.

"Leave me alone," he said without moving his mouth.

"Do you want something to eat? That might perk you up."

"No."

"Is it something I said or . . . ."

"Go away."

He didn't attend classes the next day. During the whole weekend, he stayed in bed, staring at the ceiling. Now what? The meltdown shocked me. I didn't have any idea where to turn. He couldn't possibly go to school in this condition. Should I go to the Dean of Students? I couldn't ask my parents for help or advise. They'd tell me it all happened because I stopped going to church. I felt alone, inadequate.

On Tuesday, only two days of classes missed, Harold forced himself out of bed. When he came home, he couldn't talk. He collapsed on the living room floor.

Three weeks later, he acted almost normal. However, there was no glint in his eye. He spoke quietly but at least he spoke.

"I guess you overdid," I said. "Did you see the depression coming?"

"Depression? That's what you think? I got a bug or something. I'm not depressive."

"One thing to consider, Harold, I'm tired all the time, too. We've been vegetarians for years now—you far longer. Maybe we lack something in our diet. Weren't you supposed to get a physical before you started medical school? I thought that had been a requirement."

"I put it off. Remember those exams I had to complete? I received an extension than I just forgot about it. No one said anything."

"Now's the time. I want to be checked out too. I can't go on being this exhausted. I use my lunch hour to crawl into a dark spot and sleep. We're too young to feel like this."

Laboratory reports came back showing both of us with severe anemia.

"The doctor said it amazed him that either of us could function," Harold told me. "God, I feel so much better understanding what happened." Relief flooded his face "It was all diet. Diet, for goodness sake. That's my specialty and I never considered it." He gave me a bear hug, lifting me off the floor.

"Now what?" I asked. "We know the problem. What's the cure."

"Fish. We're going to be big time fish eaters. We'll be well in no time. Watch out world, I'm coming."

# Chapter Fifty

Harold walked down our steep cellar steps, pencil behind his ear, a sheaf of papers in his hand. He started talking to me before I turned around.

"Our lab reports show just what I expected. We're back to normal in less than six months. Lack of protein did us in. Now we're a couple of super healthy young adults.

"Yeah, I know that." I turned away from the laundry tub, waiting to hear what this unexpected visit could be about. Harold didn't venture into the cellar except every month to turn the levers on the big metal posts that slowly straightened our little home.

"This is the thing, Karlan. I don't want you to wait any longer to have a child. I'm sure your anemia didn't help you during your other pregnancies and . . ."

"Wait a minute. Where is this coming from? I'm not going to be a mother and work ten hours a day."

"Of course not. That's what I've been figuring. After the baby comes, you stay home for the first six months then work part-time."

"And we live on what?"

"We borrow more. I've talked to the powers that be. My grades are good. More money is available."

"Why don't you ever talk to me about stuff until after you've decided?"

"Because you'd ask all these questions and I needed to have answers. So do you want to make a baby?"

One of the important details Harold had worked out was finding a great obstetrician. "He specializes in 'habitual aborters,'" Harold told me. "His success rate is phenomenal. One problem, though, all his patients fall in love with him. Can you handle the temptation?"

"If he's as good as you say, I'll promise to love him forever. At least if he gives us a baby."

Prematurely gray with eyes the color of Oregon lakes, Dr. Harper lived up to his reputation of being "gorgeous."

"Of course, you can have a child," he told me when I went in for my first appointment. "I want you to live a normal life, see me every two weeks. And start buying baby clothes. It's going to happen."

Dr. Harper amazed me. He didn't give me tea and cookies but he treated me like some sort of queen. When I sat on the edge of the examining table, he didn't say, "now lie back." He lifted my legs moving them onto the table while he cradled my head. It felt like a total body caress. I looked up at his nurse who smiled sweetly, then gave me a discreet wink. She knew this guy overwhelmed his patients. Everything about him soothed. I felt like a remarkable petri dish that contained some precious substance he would protect with all his skill.

On most visits, we just talked, going over diet, sleep habits, any possible stress. Warmth, safety surrounded me.

"You're unusually focused, Karlan. You're going to have this child."

Of course I would. I stopped checking to see if I had bled in the last hour. I relaxed and enjoyed my body expanding into wonderment. I worked full time up to the moment my water broke.

With Harold at my side, a nurse wheeled me to the delivery room. Just when we got to the door, Harold fainted. Quickly, everyone went to him. I waited in serene calm until someone remembered a baby was coming. I had natural childbirth. I wanted to be part of every moment. A breech birth brought pain but my body exploded in ecstasy when our child entered the world. With baby Richard on my chest, Dr. Harper wheeled me into a storage closet.

"This family needs a little alone time," he announced to the staff.

He closed the three of us inside. The only light came from a crack under the door. Harold sobbed. Our son screamed. I cheered, then blissfully fell asleep.

# Chapter Fifty-One

We called our second son "the miracle child." He came to us during Harold's internship year. Two-and-a-half-year-old, Rick didn't like the idea of sharing his parents.

"No," he told us when we spoke about another child. "Go away, baby."

Our plans were to adopt. "We're in no hurry," I told Harold. "Let's give Rick another couple of years."

We knew we would be adopting because when Harold worked on the pediatric floor during his final year of medical school, he contracted mumps. Sick as a dog, with a high fever, he had to continue on rounds. The resident in charge didn't care how he felt.

"Wear a mask," the doctor said. "Physicians have to learn to work 'hurt.'"

Maybe Harold would have developed mumps orchitis even if he went straight to bed but lack of rest didn't help. Harold's condition became so severe, he landed in the hospital. Few were surprised when he ended up sterile.

Nine months after our "little talk" with Rick, I gave birth to Robert Morgan Styler. We celebrated the wonder of him. But Harold's killing schedule eroded our joy. I watched him slowly deteriorate. Often he doubled over with chest pains. No cause could be found. He looked five years older. Depression became his constant companion.

When Stanford accepted him for a residency in allergy and immunology, we knew better days lay ahead. Rick was responsible for Harold's choice of specialty. Our first born could only eat lamb, soy milk and pears. While I nursed, I couldn't deviate from that diet or our beloved son would be covered in seeping welts. The more Harold tried to help him, the more intrigued he became with the field.

We still struggled financially though we were able to buy a small track home with an oversized backyard. I applied for a child care license. If I worked at home, I could be with Rick, now four, and Rob, one. But four more children, ages two and three, seemed to multiply by ten. I had dreams of serene walks to the park, happy picnic lunches, preschool preparation, story-time followed by long naps. Instead, I had chaos. Our boys resented sharing me, Harold came home dead tired to a house upside down.

One little girl, Betty Ann, had been coming for a about a month. She arrived one Monday morning with a large untreated injury on her hand.

"When did this happen?" I asked her.

"Ahh, when I got home . . . . after, after, I be here."

"On Friday, then. It looks very sore, Betty Ann. Does it hurt?"

"Ah-ha. It hurt big."

"How did it happen?"

"Momma say no tell."

I couldn't reach her mother. Next I called Harold to see if he could come home for lunch. No question, the gouged out wound had become infected. Harold couldn't ignore a kid in pain. When he had been a student, the nurses told me, he never left a baby with a dirty diaper. He spent quality moments with the sick, not just treating but communicating one-on-one.

"If I don't have time to look into a patient's eyes and see a person," he said, "I'm not a physician."

Harold placed Betty Ann's swollen hand on a sterile pad.

"You doctor?" she asked him, her dark eyes full of innocence. "Momma not let grandma fix me. Momma say, 'doctor do it.'" She paused looking at Harold thoughtfully.

"Momma say," Betty Ann started giggling. "Momma say she 'sue you pants off.'"

Harold waited for Betty Ann's mother to pick her up. Meanwhile he contacted the children's welfare office to report child abuse.

"Oh, children say the damnedest things," insisted Betty Ann's mother.

We said good-by to Betty Ann and took out a hefty insurance policy.

After three years of the hardest job I ever had, we figured I cleared less than fifty cents an hour.

# Chapter Fifty-Two

I couldn't afford a new dress so decided to make one. Patience had never been my long suit. I wrecked the first try. The kids giggled while I ripped it apart in disgust.

"Damn it, Harold, I should have bought a dress. Decent material is way too expensive, particularly when you buy it twice."

"And so was the sewing machine," he groused. "You said it would save us money."

Harold looked grumpy. I shouldn't have told him about my dress disaster. The one I finally finished, looked pretty good. I modeled it proudly.

"What do you think? What do you think?" I swished back and forth.

"I think I don't want to go to this stupid dinner." He looked at me but didn't smile. "Your dress is fine but I'd much rather eat at home."

"Well, we've accepted. You called it a 'command performance.' Remember? Oh, cheer up, Harold. Lois is a gourmet cook. Besides, you know everybody."

"That's the trouble, too many people."

"I'm looking forward to it. I get tired of cooking all the time. And, I like getting dolled up for once." I sashayed into the bedroom dreaming of a glorious night out.

What a gala feast, even better than I expected. I kept track of Harold. I relaxed when I saw him laughing with one of the guests.

We had finished the rock cornish game hens stuffed with corn bread, oranges, and pecans. I tried to figure out the ingredients that went into the spectacular cranberry chutney. This was the kind of meal I'd remember.

We were waiting for coffee and dessert when Lois tapped her wine glass with a spoon. "I don't know if all of you have met our daughter, Virginia."

The eleven-year-old came bouncing in full of enthusiasm. Her hair had been pulled up on top of her head with a bright green ribbon. Her curls looked like a volcano of golds and reds spilling to her shoulders. She walked right up to Harold's chair.

"Virginia's been in Stuttgart for the summer with my brother's family," Lois announced.

With a big smile, Virginia began speaking German to Harold. He stared at her. She tried again, speaking very slowly, carefully articulating each word. Still Harold remained mute, his mouth hanging open. I didn't know how to help him. I saw a subtle tremor take over his body.

"What in the world's the matter with you?" the host demanded.

Harold's face flushed. He made a sound more like a moan than a word. Virginia looked close to tears. Her father jumped up. He started to move toward his daughter then stopped. He looked at Harold and spoke with intensity. All twelve guests stared riveted.

"You talked to a German patient of mine whose English I couldn't understand. You were able to do that. Why can't you speak to my daughter? Even I can understand her German."

Harold left the table without a word.

I tried to explain. "It surprised him, don't you see? He didn't have time to prepare. You can't understand his, well, his history. German is connected to so much pain for him."

I went over to Virginia, put my arm around her. I talked to her in my rusty German. We spoke a few phases. She smiled but still looked bewildered.

"I think Harold must be ill," I said quietly. "I'm sorry to leave so suddenly."

I found Harold in the car, hunched over, crying.

# Chapter Fifty-Three

My husband turned into a different person when we hosted a party. I looked forward to having friends over. Harold seemed relaxed, pleased with the comments about my cooking. But he didn't notice subtle seasonings or special dishes. He had to be told he was eating gourmet food.

"That was a terrific meal tonight," he said once. "All our guests commented."

"But did you enjoy it?"

"It's strange, Karlan, but everything tastes the same. I guess I'd know if it were bad—too salty or something but, well, I don't know what to tell you."

How I wished I could find some way to help him enjoy life. I longed to have him interact with our children—actually play with them but instead he was a benign observer. When I romped with the boys or read stories, Harold wanted to be in the same room with us, sitting in his big chair, a stack of medical journals piled at his side. The warmth of his look when he glanced our way charmed me. I felt he gave us what he could.

One fall evening after we'd had dinner, the television repairman came. A young, robust fellow, he whispered when he walked in the door.

"I'm sorry to disturb you," he apologized.

Baroque music played softly on the hi-fi. The boys and I, deep into make-believe, stretched out on the floor with a four-foot-high castle handmade by Uncle Bob.

The repairman put down his tool kit, stared at us. He didn't move for a couple of minutes. "This is the way a family should be," he said in awe. "In my house the television is blaring; my wife's yelling to turn it down; the kids are fighting; I'm trying to fix the broken faucet and grouching. You people know how to live."

Both boys looked up at him, blinking.

"Ah, wait a minute," I said. "This is rare. Our kids chase each other. I'm always yelling for them to be careful. You caught us at a unique moment of peace. Remember, our television's not working."

After he left, Harold looked at me with disappointment.

"Why did you spoil it? It felt so good being a family to envy."

"We are a family to envy, Harold." I put my arms around him. "We're just not a peaceful family—at least not most of the time. You hate false pretenses."

The next morning, barely past dawn, all four of us took to the tennis courts. With no one else around, the boys whacked balls at will in the court next to us. Harold and I fell into our usual routine.

"All I ask, Karlan, is that you move your feet. Just that, move your feet. You look like you're trapped in cement."

I did a jig, moving my feet in all directions while balls whisked by. This caught our sons' attention. They cheered me on.

"See, I'm moving my feet," I taunted.

"All right, all right, just three things then: look at the ball, pull your racket back with the expectation you might actually hit something, and move your damn feet."

We left the court in mutual frustration. Certainly not a peaceful morning but we didn't give up. We played whenever we could. I took lessons for years but improvement was scratchy. I knew Harold dreamed of the day I excelled in something important to him. I could imagine his frustration and yet, I put my energies into relishing the moment at hand.

Harold rode himself far harder then he did me. He rarely enjoyed "almost good'" but demanded perfection for himself. He never pressured his sons—ever. When we learned Rick suffered from dyslexia just like me, Harold became pro-active.

Rick's first-grade teacher told us, "He's the only child I ever had who literally climbed the walls."

"Poor baby." I shook my head trying to figure how to save him from being miserable in school. "He got my whole syndrome. He sees letters backwards, he's hyperactive and can't focus. At least he doesn't have hallucinations."

"Not 'poor Rick.'" Harold had that purposeful look in his eye. "Like you, he's smart and he has us for parents. I'll talk to everyone: teacher, principal, school counselor. We're not going to repeat history."

I loved this side of Harold: the fighter, the righter of wrongs, the one who solved difficult challenges.

Rob had struggles as well: an inadequate immune system. Harold's expertise in immunology made all the difference in Rob's young life. Microbes most of us handle with ease, threatened Rob's life. Harold wouldn't let him be hospitalized but tended him at home.

"Kids get scars from long hospital stays." Harold talked to me quietly outside Rob's door. "Besides, too many come down with exotic infections from being in a hospital. I'm not spending enough time with the boys but I can give them my best medical know-how." He consulted every expert available, celebrating when Rob once again bounced back into health.

We couldn't be described as a peaceful family but in difficult times, we knew how to pull together.

# Chapter Fifty-Four

Harold hated cold. It had been the main reason we left Michigan for California. Warmth seemed to make his brain work better. He liked to sit in a tub of hot water to do his thinking. I often joined him in consultation, sitting on a stool beside him. These were special moments. The kids knew to leave us alone.

"Karlan, I've got some ideas. Only half-backed but they have to do with research being done by another physician. I'm only a resident. Maybe I shouldn't say anything."

"Why not? What could be the problem?"

"I don't want to come across as interfering. He's finished with his residency. Maybe I'll seem pushy."

"I hope that's not what medicine's about. If you can't share ideas, nothing will move forward."

"That's what I used to think. But there's a lot of jealousy and ego, not the intellectual openness I expected. I guess it comes down to doing what feels right to me."

"I like you this way," I told him, "reflective, energized with ideas but not . . . well, bouncing off the wall." I looked to see if I had pinched a nerve.

"When else do you like me?"

The question surprised me. He looked up with eager eyes, like a kid, vulnerable, hoping.

"I like you all the time."

"No, no, that's not what I mean. Besides, it's not true. You don't like me when I'm criticizing you. Lots of times I can tell you wish I'd get lost."

"I like you for not riding our sons."

We stayed quiet.

"Remember, Harold, when you said you wanted them 'protected in life by the cloak of self love'? I liked the man who said that. I think, for your sake, you should play more, not just with them but with me, too. You're a special father, a wonderful physician and you've done so much for me." I let quiet engulf us again. "I appreciate that you don't interfere with my storytelling, my make-believe."

"Of course not. Why would I do that? It's wonderful. I wish . . . ."

"Harold, tell the doctor about your ideas. I can't think of any reason not to."

Two weeks later, Harold told me about his conversation with Dr. Franklin. "It felt strange, Karlan. The guy never looked at me. He asked how I acquired the translations. I told him I spoke the languages. He made this funny dismissive sound as if . . . I don't know, maybe he didn't think they could be worth anything." Harold sat on his favorite chair looking befuddled. "When I told him my specific idea, he pulled out his pen, wrote it down but then he just walked away. Oh, well. No harm done."

Almost two years passed. Harold had nearly finished his residency when he received a summons from his supervisor, Dr. Barker. Harold told me the ugly details. His face looked as drained as when he described his teacher's death at the hands of the brown coats.

"He called me an intellectual thief," Harold spoke in a whisper. "Dr. Baker . . . he told me Dr. Franklin said I was stealing his research . . . wanted credit. Dr. Baker looked at me as if I were a criminal."

"But you told him what happened, Right? You didn't let . . . ."

"I . . . I said I had approached Dr. Franklin to give him some information . . . save him time. I had an idea but no place to go with it. I thought . . . I had hoped it would help him."

"Then what did Dr. Baker say to that?"

"What he said, Karlan, his exact words: 'You disgust me. Just because you haven't lived up to your potential, you have to look impressive through the efforts of someone else. We expected great things from you but you're a washout, get out of here.'"

I put my arms around him but couldn't think how to comfort him.

"Do you think if I told Dr. Baker that I . . . about our conversation when you were in the tub, I mean."

'No, Karlan. That wouldn't help." Harold put his head in his hands. When he looked up after several minutes, his color had returned.

"Research is such a different world than I thought. And you know, I am a washout. Everything I come up with is half-backed. I dreamed of being . . . I thought I could help asthmatics. I still think I can be a good physician but not in . . . ."

"I still don't get it," I interrupted. "Of what have you been accused? I thought you never talked to Dr. Franklin after that first conversation."

"Oh, I tried to speak to him. I saw him in the halls, in the cafeteria. He always seemed to avoid me. He never made eye contact."

"Explain this to me. How could anyone accuse you of anything?"

"Karlan, his thesis turned out to be pretty much what I suggested to him. He did the work proving the idea, refining it. It's his work. I never thought otherwise but . . . when the synopsis of his research came out in print, he probably felt insecure. Maybe he figured if he attacked me first, he'd be safe."

"Harold, you have to fight. Explain what happened. Show Dr. Barker the translations you did and your notes."

"For about ten minutes, Karlan, I fought back, quietly, calmly. You should have seen Dr. Barker's face. He sneered. I just wanted to get out of his office."

Harold gave up all interest in research. He picked a medium sized medical group in Santa Barbara.

A month before we moved, Harold put an envelope on my breakfast mat. Inside were two round-trip tickets to Europe.

"Time for that honeymoon," he said.

# Chapter Fifty-Five

I cried halfway to Europe.

"Oh, give me a break, Karlan. The boys aren't missing you half as much as you do them. They were excited. They both have a friend their age and it's hardly an adjustment. They're in the Williams's house as much as ours."

"I know you're right. They just looked so little, waving as we drove away. But okay, I'm done."

We couldn't afford this trip. Harold borrowed the money. He said we needed a break.

"I just want to be alone with you for a couple of weeks. I'm not complaining about how much time you spend with Rick and Rob but I feel, sometimes, I'm an overload—like you wish I weren't there."

"Yeah? That's no fun. I don't like you feeling that way. There are times I hunger to be alone. Just by myself with no one wanting anything from me. You know that feeling. Don't you have it sometimes?"

"Yes! And, okay. I hear you. I can do something about that. Once I start at Sansum clinic, we'll have enough money so you can take a weekend off every now and then. Be all by yourself."

"You mean it? You won't feel deserted?"

"I'll work on my feelings. You work on yours."

Our days tumbled into each other but the warm, honest exchange felt better than at any other time in our marriage.

At the beginning of our second week, we went climbing in the Bavarian Alps. It started as a gorgeous day for a hike. I wore shorts, a tee shirt, sockless sneakers plus a sweater tied around my waist. Harold didn't want to get too much sun so he wore long pants.

"Gosh, you look bundled up for a warm afternoon. At least undo the top button on your shirt and roll up your sleeves. If you want to relax, you have to look the part."

"Want me relaxed, huh? I'll show you relaxed. Look what's to your left. Give you any ideas?"

He had spotted a little island of grass in the middle of a mound of rocks. It reminded him of our special place in Provo.

"I think this has been used for picnics," I said. "Here's a spoon. Probably other treasures if we look carefully."

"Quit scavenging and come here, Karlan. We're totally private."

Harold took my sweater for a shared pillow. We made slow love then fell asleep in each other's arms. We awoke to snow falling on our faces.

"What's happened? Harold, it's freezing. Isn't this May?"

Harold looked disoriented, his hair disheveled. His teeth began to chatter.

"How long have we slept? Good God, Karlan, it's four o'clock. No wonder we're cold. Let's get to the car."

Harold took my hand. Neither of us noticed my sweater left behind. We were both dazed. Harold seemed in charge but didn't know where to go. He went in one direction and then another.

"With no sun, I can't tell where we are. Why didn't I bring a compass?"

We had walked briskly for about a half-an-hour.

"Where's our car? It should be right here." Harold turned in circles. "We didn't walk any further than this, did we? Maybe we're going in the wrong direction?"

I wasn't worried. Everything seemed just as it should—like a fairy tale.

"This is the right road, Harold, but our car got swallowed up by something." That seemed like a logical explanation. Harold looked hard at me. I smiled back at him.

"Karlan, where's your shoe?" He sounded strange. "You're walking in snow. When did you lose your shoe? Didn't you have a sweater? Lord, you're freezing."

Harold pulled me into his lap, rubbed my cold foot. I couldn't feel anything. He wrapped me in his arms.

"You know what I want, Harold? I want to sleep. It's going to be okay. If we just sleep for a little while, the sun will come out. Then we can find the car."

"How could you get . . . so fast . . . . Okay, I'll carry you on by back."

Harold stopped periodically to rub my foot, to catch his breath. His puffing sounded like a laboring machine far off in the distance. At some point, he put his sock on my foot. I remember sleeping in his arms, not wanting him to rouse me.

I didn't like him sharply talking to me, right in my ear. "Come on, Karlan, help me. Stand on that rock so I can get you on my back." I lost track of time. I came alert when Harold jerked to a stop.

"Look, I see a light down there. Finally, thank God. I thought I might be walking in circles."

"Where? Where's a light" I don't see anything. Everything's black."

"Down in that copse of trees. I'm going to leave you here and get some help. Don't move. No matter what, don't move."

The farmer came back with Harold pushing a wheelbarrow. When I got to the farm, they put my foot in cold water. It felt hot to me. The pain when my foot began to come to life brought me awake in a hurry. We spent the night in the cozy farm house. I couldn't eat dinner but felt much better by morning, I gobbled all the breakfast offered.

"What an adventure to tell the kids."

"Adventure—near disaster. If we hadn't found the farm house, you might have lost some toes. You must be susceptible to hypothermia. You went down hill so fast, you scared me."

I remembered the incident as a glorious time of abandoned lovemaking. The rest just seemed a dream. Harold filled in all the gaps of my memory. It felt like someone else's story.

On the plane back home, Harold and I talked about our hunger to have a daughter. We saw our trip as a new beginning. Adopting a little girl would make a perfect family.

# Chapter Fifty-Six

"What do you think about having a sister?" Harold asked the boys.

"What?" Rob looked confused, upset.

"You pregnant, mom? How do you know it's a girl?" Rick, the sophisticated one, had a smile on his face, eying my abdomen.

"I can't get pregnant anymore." I sat on the floor, gathered my sons into my lap. "We'll adopt a little girl. What do you think?"

"Wow," said Rick.

Rob pulled away, frowning. This wasn't going the way I wanted. Clearly Harold, the trained psychologist-physician, had come on too strong. But he didn't see it. He sparkled with excitement.

"Your sister might come from China or India or maybe be an American Indian or even Black. Would that matter to you? Would it bother you if she had something wrong with her?" asked Harold as if suggesting a picnic.

"Why do you want a girl with something wrong with her?" Rob now looked clearly worried.

"Because those children have a harder time being placed into a good home. Their spirits are the same. They need loving just like you two. It's not their fault they were born with a problem like a club foot or a hair lip. We could do everything medically possible to fix the problem."

That night while we lay in bed, I took Harold's hand. "Don't say anything more for a couple of weeks. Let this bomb shell get absorbed. Let them bring it up. It's not going to happen for a long time."

"With two children, we'll be on the bottom of the list." Harold sounded let down.

"Bottom of the list! After we tell the adoption agency about our challenges, we'll be on a sheet filed in a locked drawer."

"What do you mean?"

"Well, I'm still in therapy and you've had depressive episodes."

"But we're good parents. And you haven't had any serious problems for years."

"Yes, but I'm going to be completely honest about who we are."

We told "all" to the agency.

"We appreciate your candor," said Mrs. Blackwood, the social worker. "We'll need statements from your psychiatrists, from your neighbors, several friends who are not family. There will be a long wait." I thought her rather cold for the kind of work she did.

We stopped listening for the phone to ring. Rick and Rob ceased asking questions. The call came two years after all the paper work had been submitted.

"She's seven-weeks-old," said Mrs. Blackwood. "A premature birth. She looks perfect but she . . . she's not thriving." A long pause came next.

"What? What do you think might be . . . wrong?" My hands began to sweat.

"I shouldn't be calling you without the final medical release." The social worker sounded close to tears. "I know, not in my mind but in my heart, that this child will be fine if she can just . . . go home." She didn't sound like the woman I had met. "Tracy's been in four foster homes. Just bad luck, really. Illness in the families, that sort of thing."

"Tracy?"

"Oh, dear, I'm so befuddled. I shouldn't have told you the name her birth mother gave her. You can change it, of course." Could this be the same Mrs. Blackwood who interviewed us?

"Tell me why she needs constant care?"

"She . . . doesn't seem interested in suckling a bottle. She doesn't cry much at all. But Dr. Styler can give her the medical . . . the two of you would be the perfect home. Besides, the mother read all the applications. She chose you. She calls me everyday asking if her daughter has gone 'home.' It breaks my heart."

"The biological mother knows who we are?"

"Oh, no, no. We don't do that unless you both request it at a later date. We give the applications and the letters of endorsement without names." I heard her deep intake of breath. "Please come see her. Then you decide. I'm frightened for Tracy."

Harold and I drove to the agency without speaking. Our hands shook as we held on to each other.

Mrs. Blackwood met us at the door. "Tracy gained a little weight at first but during the last few weeks she's lost weight."

We walked into an empty room with just a bassinet. Way at the bottom of the bed lay a tiny baby. At seven weeks, she looked a newborn.

She had amazing eyes that slightly slanted up and held a color I hadn't seen before. Something between green and blue but with an intensity that held me. She had a bright red puffy birthmark on her forehead. Gently I picked her up.

"You wonderful spirit. You're my daughter. I'd have known you anywhere."

Harold held her, kissing her over and over again. Then he began to examine her.

"Don't, Harold. I just want to go home with her. Don't examine her. Remember she doesn't have to be perfect. She's ours." I could feel hysteria building in me. Harold was acting like a physician.

"Karlan, she stopped urinating yesterday. Her kidneys have shut down. We have to know why so we can treat her. Dye has to be put into her system so we can look at the kidneys."

"Okay, okay, I understand that. We have to find out but we take her home. We bring her to the hospital and I hold her while these . . . these things are being done to her."

"No, because you've already bonded . . . and if . . . well, I hate to say the words, but if the tests show she won't live but a few more months, I'm not going to let you or the boys go through that."

"Harold, give me my daughter."

"Oh, God, I've done a terrible thing." Mrs. Blackwood stood at the door. Harold wouldn't give Tracy back to me. I pulled Mrs. Blackwood into my arms and held her.

"You did exactly right. Harold and I are both this child's . . . what is the word . . . advocate, champion, parent. We're going to get her home."

I sat by the phone all the next day waiting for the results. The doctor called Harold at his office. He raced home with the news that our baby had two healthy kidneys.

"Get the boys. This is it. We're getting her this minute."

When we walked in, I could see Tracy had cried. Her eyes were red rimmed, her face swollen.

"She didn't like the test," said Mrs. Blackwood. "But I cheered because she screamed. It . . . it was so normal and . . . and strong."

Rick went right up to her ready to carry her home himself. Rob held back but finally asked to hold her, too.

"What color are those eyes?" asked Rick.

"Azure," answered her proud father. Harold hadn't stopped beaming. Tracy kept tracking me, even when the boys held her. But she stayed quiet. She made mewing sounds.

"What are we going to name her?" Rob asked.

"Tra . . ." I started to say the name I had been using in my mind but Harold interrupted me.

"How do you like, 'Kendra?'"

I had never heard him mention the name, "Kendra." We had talked of several possibilities. I liked, "Lynn", for my cousin. Maybe "Joan" for my sister. And then I settled on "Tracy."

"Where did, 'Kendra,' come from?" I asked.

"I knew a girl by that name," Harold told us. "When I was about fifteen. She was the most beautiful creature I had ever seen. She had eyes like . . . like our baby." Harold gently took her from Rob, cradling her in his arms. "I told myself, if the test came through okay, she would be our 'Kendra.'"

"Hi, Kendra," said Rick

"How about Kendra Lynn?" suggested Harold.

So it was.

Instinctively, I wrapped my body in a big bathrobe, the top half of me naked. I put Kendra's bare body against me in a sling. I held her almost constantly with just a loose diaper under her. I slept with her, fed her as often as she'd accept a few drops. Harold cheered my instinctive healing methods.

"Come alive, little one, you're safe now," I whispered.

# *Chapter Fifty-Seven*

"Karlan, you can give our baby more by not being exhausted. Accept help." Harold sounded firm. "Kendra's made great strides. So relax, already." His face softened. "Another point, I want to see you once in awhile—so do the boys."

He'd found an ideal baby-sitting couple. But I had chaffed when I met Bobby. She seemed so perfect, so qualified. I felt incompetent. Bobby and her husband, both retired, took joy in children. They had a relaxed, cheerful home. I kept looking for something wrong. Surely no one could be as good for my little girl as I was.

Finally, I gave in. We would all be better off with Bobby in our lives. Once a week, Kendra went to a child's Shangri-la. On the Saturdays she was gone, I did something special with Rick and Rob.

Still, I ached with how Bobby floated without stress, while I struggled, stumbled. I couldn't get Kendra to eat but she ate everything Bobby served. Worse than that, Kendra would tug on the door, yelling: "Bobby, Bobby."

"Karlan, don't tell me you're jealous!" This came from my best friend, Janet Dunbar. "Kendra cries, 'momma, momma,' when she's with Bobby. She has you on a string." Janet looked hard at me. "This is nutty. You have no perspective. Everything is about Kendra. I'm tired of hearing what she ate, how beautiful her tantrums are. I want my friend back." Janet scowled, her dark hair tumbling over her shoulders. "I should be mad at you, but I'm resenting a little girl, for mercy's sake."

"Janet, I asked you to have lunch with me to make me feel better. I don't have things in balance but I'm working on it so let up, will you?" Janet pressed her lips together. "Okay, for now."

"Did I tell you mother's coming for a visit?" I wanted to change the subject.

"How are you going to handle that one." Janet looked friendlier.

"I'm going to make a schedule. Mother's visit isn't going to undo me. Friday, I'll clean the house, Saturday will be for groceries, Sunday I'll do the yard."

"And what happens when your mother runs her finger over the top of the refrigerator and comes up with dirt?"

"Sunday night, I clean the top of the refrigerator."

Janet reached for my arm. "You've cleaved Kendra to your hip. It's not good for either of you. While you're getting ready for your mother, let her stay at Bobby's house."

"Okay." I went home with resolve.

"Harold, will you stack your papers into some kind of order so I can dust around them—please?" I could hear from my voice that calmness hadn't arrived with the making of a schedule.

"Forget about the dust, Karlan. My papers aren't to be touched. This is our house. We're going to be gracious to your mother but not turn our lives upside down."

Kendra tottered into the room then dropped down and crawled the rest of the way to where Harold stood. Almost three, Kendra still liked crawling. It was faster and safer. She had no trouble getting around or making her needs known. She reached up to her daddy. His face broke into sunlight.

"Are you happy your grandma's coming for a visit?" He picked her up then slow waltzed around the room. "I'm glad you took Janet's advice," he told me. "You're altogether too tense about this visit. Kendra will be better off with Bobby." He gave me a one armed hug, cradling our daughter with the other. "I'll drop Kendra off on my way to the office."

I stayed on schedule, the menu planned, flowers everywhere. Dust in the living room continued to keep Harold's papers company. Rick and Rob played outside like I asked. But I had felt strange when I woke up Saturday morning, dizzy, apprehensive. Could it be because my baby so cheerfully went to Bobby's house?—went to Bobby without looking back?

I started scrubbing the kitchen floor. Rick and Rob came in for milk and graham crackers. Full of good spirits, they started wrestling, then grunting. They slammed doors, just like usual. Slam! Slam! Slam!

I started to say, "Stop that. You're driving me crazy" but I didn't get the words out. Suddenly, in my mind, I saw myself grab them by the back of the neck, whack their heads together. My imagination created their skulls exploding like terra cotta pottery. The fantasy so vivid, I could hear their heads crack. I couldn't breath. Who was this? What kind of monster could see herself hurt her babies. How could it happened? I kept rage hidden in zip lock bags. I stumbled to the phone, got through to Harold. He left his patient, took a private line.

"It's okay. You're okay. Just overloaded. I'll cancel your mother. What you need are a few days . . . . no, more like a week—a safe retreat. Let me think. I got it, Esalen. I'll set it up."

"Harold?"

"Shhh, it will be fine. There's been too much confusion. You won't have to do anything but get massages, swim, sleep. Karlan, we all have crazy thoughts. It's not acting on them that makes us civilized. You're okay. You're a great mother. I'll be home in an hour."

I sank into gratitude. I took a deep breath, called the boys.

"Hey guys, it's hard on me when you slam doors. I don't know why it bothers me so much but it seems to just about make me sick. So, please, knock it off."

"Is it because grandma's coming?" asked Rick.

"No, Rick, it's not grandma's fault. I've always had trouble with doors slamming. But because I've let things pile on top of each other lately, I'm not my best self. Little things are bothering me more than they should. By the way, your father's canceled grandma's visit. Your father and I look out for each other."

# Chapter Fifty-Eight

Four days later found me heading up the coast.

Esalen had all the wonders of a natural paradise. Too much, I couldn't take it in. Maybe no one would notice how out of place I felt. Whose body was this? Didn't like myself much. Didn't know what to do about it.

I passed the open doors of a huge ballroom with earthy music pouring out. A firm hand with rows of silver bracelets grabbed my arm.

"In here girl. Feel the beat and just move." I smelled jasmine as she grinned up at me. "Ugh," her face turned to a grimace. "First take off those dumb shoes. Then let yourself flow."

I shook my head, pulled back. It felt like the time I took ballet lessons—awkward, stupid. Another set of hands took hold me, pulled me fast around the perimeter. When did I start skipping? Someone twirled me. I became part of the whole. Finally, breathless, I staggered to the door, laughing without knowing it. I headed to the reception desk for my key, ready to let the place do its magic.

When I unlocked my door, another woman lay stretched out on one of the twin beds. Attractive, about my age, she had streaked blond hair with dramatic eye makeup. She smiled up at me.

"Surprise! They overbooked, so you get a roomy. I'm Patricia." She went on filing her nails. "You'll hardly know I'm here. This place has me packed solid with workshops and meetings. I don't know when I'm going to sleep." She batted her lashes. Her white teeth made me blink.

"Patricia, I hate sounding inflexible but I absolutely need to be alone. See, I'm escaping confusion. That's why I came. I'll . . . I'll talk to someone."

She shook her head. "If you check the fine print, it tells you these rooms are booked for two whenever necessary."

She had it right. Damn!

"Okay, but let's give each other as much privacy as possible. I'll try not to be a grouch. It isn't your fault."

I wandered down twisting paths that ended in gardens with deep pools holding multicolor koi. The solitude, what I had longed for, left me disjointed. It took the hot tubs to turn me around. Several large stone baths, each a different temperature, sat solidly on the cliff lip. The ocean thundered below. Mineral waters soothed my body. The rhythmic crashing of waves calmed my soul. Now I could manage anything. I had a leisurely dinner, took another long walk, went to bed.

Deeply asleep, my dream disintegrated with a frantic hiss.

"Karlan, get up. You have to get out of here. I need the room."

"What are you talking about?" I struggled to orient myself.

"It's a matter of my life! You have to do this for me. Quick, he's just peeing. He'll be here any moment. I told him I had the room to myself. Go through the window."

"I'm not going through any window!"

"My God, this is my life. Weren't you ever young and in love?"

"Oh, what crap!"

I gathered up my pants, shirt, went through the door. I almost knocked over Mr. Wonderful. After going a couple of steps, it hit me: no shoes. I walked around feeling like a loser—embarrassed, then enraged. First my mother manipulated me, my kids abused me, Harold tried to change me.

Now a stranger pushed me out of my room. I stumbled through the dark, freezing. Finally, I headed back and sat near the cabin until almost dawn. After "Casanova" took his leave, I stormed back into the room, only to find it empty. What happened to Patricia? Had I stayed out in the cold so her lover could sleep tight?

I didn't see her until the next day. She stood in the middle of the room throwing her clothes into a backpack.

"I'm going to sue this place," she said in a rage. "They fill it with predators that just laugh in your face. Therapist my foot. Lying user, more like it. I probably have herpes. He hurt me and wouldn't even leave."

I swallowed my irritation. She got the worst of the deal. By the time I left, it became a funny story. Most important, Patricia taught me plenty about myself. I didn't have to be pushed around. I could make choices. My heart felt light.

# Chapter Fifty-Nine

When I got home, I noticed subtle changes in Harold. My overload must have blinded me. I was used to his criticism but now he found fault with everyone—everyone but his three children. In the past Harold had a wealth of understanding for others, making allowances, extending a generous heart.

No more. His sourness leaked into every part of his life, seeping into our home like a poison. His discontent grew, gathering strength. Trades people didn't want to come to our house because of his caustic comments. He scolded colleagues for not knowing drug interactions. He made enemies of surgeons by challenging them for being too quick to operate. He appointed himself watchdog regarding ethical revenue. He stepped on toes. His sharp mind became his adversary.

Harold had helped rescue me from my crisis, now I had a chance to repay him. I planned my strategy carefully.

"Do you remember telling me about Dr. Semmelweis?" Harold and I sat together on our screened in porch enjoying a simple dinner. The children had overnights with friends. Next week it would be our turn to have a house full of kids.

"What about him?" he asked.

"You said he figured out that germs were killing women in the maternity wards. But when his colleagues wouldn't wash their hands, he went crazy. Remember telling me that?"

Harold put down his fork, smiled at me. He knew where I was going with this story.

"You're telling me I'm like Semmelweis?"

"Not exactly. You're not throwing doctors against the wall but you're making everyone angry. That means no one will listen to you." I got up, went behind him, rubbed his shoulders. "Trouble with the Semmelweis approach, everyone fought him, hated him. And, Harold, women continued to die. If you have something important you want to get across . . ."

Harold turned to me, looked thoughtful. I felt on a roll. I hadn't planned to say anything about his father but words spilled out of my mouth before I could stop them.

"Have you thought how similar you are to your father? He'd get depressed for months, take to his bed. Then one morning, he'd wake up full of energy. You told me about it. That's when you would be the most afraid of him. He'd get a divorce, sue all his friends."

I couldn't see Harold's face. I imagined him reflecting on what I said. Instead, he leapt to his feet, knocked over the chair, his face contorted. I didn't see it coming. He struck me on the arm with such force, I flew backwards, cracking into the wall. I tried to protect my fall with my hand bending my finger. Harold glared at me.

"I'm nothing like my father. Nothing." He stormed out of the house.

I sat numb on the floor. I felt my head, saw blood on my hand. What happened? What did I say? I didn't think. He did everything for me. Took care of me, sent me to a safe place, didn't judge me, now I pushed him over the edge. It was my fault, all my fault.

I hadn't moved by the time Harold came back. He crouched in front of me. He looked at my head wound, then my finger. A strange noise came out of his throat.

"All your life, you'll have pain in that finger. You'll develop arthritis in it. And I did this to you. I'll never forgive myself."

My mind began to clear. I felt anguished for Harold. I couldn't bear to see him twisted in guilt.

"My finger will be fine, Harold. What you did . . . you flung me like garbage. I can't live with physical abuse. But, still, I shouldn't have said you were like your father. You're nothing like him. Your father would never have helped his wife as you've helped me. You're a good man."

He looked at me in confusion. "I'm nothing like him . . . that's right. I could never hit a child or a woman or hurt anyone, never, never could do such a thing."

I could only stare, my voice came out low, soothing.

"That doesn't make sense, Harold. You just hit me so you are someone who can do such a thing."

"I'm sorry. I'm sorry. You're the only person in the world I feel safe enough to give way to fury,"

"Come on, Harold." My voice sounded hard in my ears. "You were just as angry with your mother. Your face looked the same when you yelled at her as it did when you hit me. I've always been afraid of your anger. I've been careful to not push you too far. I don't dare stand up to you because I don't know what you'll do. I don't want to live in fear."

"I will never, ever, physically hurt you again."

I wanted to believe him.

# *Chapter Sixty*

I learned a few months later, physical assault doesn't damage like words quietly spoken.

We were lying together on grass at a nearby park. The day mellow, warm. We snuggled, shared our fantasies. I told Harold of all the places I would like to make love with him.

"See, I don't want to be bound by what people consider proper. I want privacy, you understand, but I want to be more . . . spontaneous. How about you?" I smiled into his eyes.

"I have a fantasy too." He sounded dreamy. "I would like to have sex, just once, with a beautiful woman."

I couldn't speak. I went into another dimension, sort of suspended, a holding pattern. I waited for my mind to catch up with my heart. In one short sentence, I saw our marriage anew. And then, a rage took hold of me. I had no space for pain. My anger drenched then left me cold, hard. When I finally spoke, my voice sounded dull.

"I know an actress," I said quietly, "another patient in my therapy group. She told me she wanted to sleep with a doctor because her father's one. She thought she might work through some of her hang-ups. She's beautiful, Harold. I'll ask her if she's interested."

Harold didn't say anything. I invited the actress for dinner, told her what Harold had said. She agreed to come. After serving dessert, I left the two alone. I went to a movie, still feeling wooden. When I came back, Harold told me she had gone shortly after I did. He seemed embarrassed.

"Wish I had gone to the movie with you," he said quietly. "Was it good?"

We never spoke of the incident. I didn't see my actress friend again. She left our group without notice.

Anger protected a wound too deep to explore. Anger kept me from seeing anyone else's pain.

# Chapter Sixty-One

We hit rock bottom a month later. Harold, in wrath, picked me up, opened the front door, and dumped me in the flower bed. I heard the lock click into place. I could hear him screaming at the walls. We had been fighting since dinner.

Now, outside and alone, I felt blissful relief. I breathed in the tender scent from our moonlit garden. What a gorgeous night to be locked out of my home.

Much too soon, I heard Harold's hurried steps. I could feel his remorse even before he spoke. He stopped in front of me, breathless.

"I'm so sorry, Karlan. I don't know what happened."

I looked at him with unexpected peace. What anger I had had drained into the grass where I sat.

"I have an idea of what happened."

"What? What, tell me?"

"You're playing an old tape, Harold. Remember when you were only seven? That would be a few years younger than Rob is now. Your father locked your mother out of the house. You called it 'the ultimate abuse,' not just to her but to you and your brother. I agreed then and now. I don't accept your apology. I won't talk about it tonight. You sleep in your office. I'm going to bed. We'll discuss it quietly tomorrow."

"You don't understand. I'm under so much pressure. I can't keep going. I need you to find some way to earn a living so I can cut back. Karlan, I'm going under."

"Harold, we talked about that earlier—for hours. We talked about it last week and the month before. I told you I'd gladly get a job but you said, 'no, no, no.' You said I had to stay home to serve you lunch every day. You want me here when the children get home from school." I sat back on the grass. I wanted the peace I had moments before. "You have a fantasy that I can make money writing children stories." I began to seethe. I took a deep breath. I didn't want more useless anger clouding my thinking.

"When you wanted to become a physician, you insisted I put off getting my degree." I stood up but stayed a couple of feet back from Harold. "I worked hard to get you through medical school. Now, you yell at me for not doing my share of paying the bills. You won't let me get a job. I have some skills. I could make enough money to give you a shorter week." I started pacing. I could feel rage coming back. I hugged myself, concentrated, tried to focus on what I wanted to say. "Harold, I have no idea what happens to your pay check. We live simply. We don't go on trips. Where—does—the—money—go? Do we have a big savings somewhere?"

He stared at me. He didn't speak for a long time. Finally, he shook his head, talking in a normal voice. He avoided my questions.

"Okay, I made a mistake. You have to hear me out. I apologize. I won't be unreasonable again. You're right. I want you here all the time. But you're so talented. You tell marvelous stories. Children would love to read them." He smiled as if I should be pleased with his compliment.

"Stop right there." I stood a foot from him now, letting my anger drench us both. Harold backed away. I gave myself time to gather my thoughts. "You know I've tried." I spit the words out at him. "I've sent in tons of stories. I can't get anything published. I've tried. Let—that—go."

"Karlan, I'm just so tired. So many people to take care of. It never stops. I hate the phone to ring."

"Not tonight, Harold. I'm tired, too. We'll talk in the morning."

# *Chapter Sixty-Two*

We ate breakfast together. I had fed the kids early. After I cleared the table, I sat in front of Harold.

"Everyone knows you're miserable. The kids know it. I know it. Our friends ask what they can do to help you. I can't make you happy. Perhaps someone else can." For once, I felt in charge. Harold stared at me. I looked calmly back at him. "Maybe, Harold, you could fall in love with a smart, professional woman. She could share your work load."

Harold's mouth hung open.

"You're asking for a divorce?" He looked thunderstruck. "You would do that to our children? I made a mistake. I said I'm sorry. Now you want to end our marriage over a mistake?"

"That's what I'm saying, Harold. Of course, I'll get a job. We can sell the house. Divide our assets." A cool calm embraced me. I sounded like I had rehearsed it all before but these thoughts came with the dawn. I had stared at the ceiling, alone in my bed, seeing a different future. I knew my life was about to get better—hard, terribly hard, but better. Even alone in the garden last night, the word, "divorce", hadn't come to my mind. I felt no panic, now.

Harold got up slowly. "You're serious, Karlan. You really mean it."

He turned around in a circle as if not knowing where to go. He began talking to himself. "Kendra will be undone. What can I tell her?" He started walking fast, heading for her room, still talking out loud. "That's right. She's not home. Thank God, I can put that off." Then he went into the playroom where the boys were engrossed in "Dungeons and Dragons." I could hear him calling our sons to him. He cried when he told them. I stayed at the table but I could hear his sobbing.

"Your mom wants to divorce me. She's going to break up our family."

I stayed put. I couldn't make out what the boys said. Then silence. I put my head down on my arms. A hand softly fell on my shoulder. When I looked up Rick and Rob stood in front of me, dry-eyed. Their faces held love, caring.

"Do we get to live with you, mom?" Rob asked.

Rick hugged my shoulders. "You're doing the right thing, mom."

After a few minutes, Harold came to where I still sat at the dining room table. He looked shocked as if he just learned the world had been flat all along. Rick got up from his seat, hugged his father.

"Dad, lots of families go through divorce. And the kids get to see their father more than when they were together. We love you. We'll see you as often as you want."

Harold kept shaking his head. I saw something horrible flood over him. I jumped up just as Harold took one end of our heavy oak table, threw it against the wall. Rick protectively pulled me behind him. Harold saw it.

"Oh, my God, my kids are afraid of me. I'd never hurt your mother, Rick, never."

"But you already have," Rob said quietly.

Harold sat down as if he had been punched. No one spoke.

"Let me talk to your mother. I'm sorry about the table. I'm okay now. I need to talk to Karlan—alone."

We talked for hours. I had care, concern for Harold but I didn't know if I loved him any more. It shocked me. I had believed my love invincible.

"Karlan, I can do better. I had no idea the boys would welcome a divorce. My God, where have I been? I won't keep saying I'm sorry. I'll show you. I've made promises before but never to you and the kids. If you'll give me another chance, I'll change."

I felt weary. I looked at his pain-filled face. An old ache pushed through my fatigue.

"There's lots of good in our marriage, Harold. We have a long history of trying, helping each other. That counts. The children love you. Rick and Rob don't want you gone. They want the misery between us gone." I took his hand. "I realized this morning that you have always been my safety net. You're there for me. But when I'm strong you attack. I don't understand the dynamics. I only know what happens between us isn't good either way."

Harold held his head, his shoulders shaking. "What I know is that I'm terrified I'll lose you if you . . . if you heal and find your balance. Yet I want that for you with all my heart."

"I believe that, Harold. If we stay together, it has to be different. We both have to commit to tough therapy. We have to face our patterns. We—we have a big responsibility not just to ourselves but to our kids."

We made an agreement to give our best efforts, risk painful therapy, see where we were in a year.

"I still think I should get a job. If this doesn't work, I'll need to earn a living."

When Harold spoke, I heard a new voice.

"Please, don't do that. If this doesn't work, I'll make sure you have the money to start again. That's another solemn promise."

Harold stopped criticizing me, cold turkey. It had been a habit built over years, nurtured by my passivity. He'd start to say something negative, then stop himself. I had a more difficult time breaking away from feeling responsible for everything, trying to fix both Harold and the kids.

Rick had a paper route. If a customer called complaining about not receiving a paper, I'd make the delivery.

"Mom, you're smothering me," my son told me. "Let me pay for my mistakes."

When Harold had a bad day, I blamed myself for saying the wrong thing, not being a strength for him.

And then there was my tension. The horrible twisting energy that took over then disappeared leaving me drained with no insight as to why it had arrived.

As the months passed, I sensed my love for Harold reawakening along with a deep admiration for his ability to change. The boys noticed the difference.

"You couldn't have helped the family more," Rick said, "than telling dad you'd had enough."

# *Chapter Sixty-Three*

Harold used his vacation time to plunge into Primal Therapy. He disappeared for three weeks. We didn't hear a word from him. I didn't like what I saw when he finally dragged himself home.

"It's so much harder than I thought. I don't know. I've never felt so rotten in my life. These people are tough. I told them about our struggles, our fights. They said you should leave me. I'm a bastard. That's what my therapist told me. I wanted someone to make me feel better but, oh, my God, Karlan, it's hard to go through this kind of therapy. What you're doing is easier. Take it slow. Be good to yourself."

Threes month later, I found an envelope on my pillow. Inside a check for ten thousand dollars and a note: "Use this for any therapy you want—but find peace. Love, Harold."

"I borrowed it," he told me. "Your spending hours in 'Reevaluation Counseling.' I see you spinning your wheels. Using lay people to unearth your problems is risky. Get real help."

"But I'm seeing a psychiatrist."

"That's the point, you see him hit and miss when you're completely overloaded. You told me yourself that half the time you talk about the problems of people you're trying to counsel. It doesn't work for you in either direction."

"I thought you said . . . well, is it Primal Therapy you hope I'll try? You called it brutal."

"I don't want you to do anything you don't want to do. Think about it, or go to a psychiatrist four times a week. Do what feels right to you." Harold walked around our bedroom looking like the walls were hemming him in. I could tell he had a lot more he wanted to say but didn't want to push me.

"Please, Harold, say what's on your mind. I'll decide but you know me so well. I trust you."

"Okay. You just skim the surface—at least that's what it looks like from here. I think "Primal Therapy" would work for you. I know, I know my results so far aren't great, but you're different than me. I hope you'll risk it."

I talked to Dr. Graham, my psychiatrist. "Give it a try," he said. "You can always quit. I'll be here if you need me. All you'll be out is money and who cares about that?"

# Chapter Sixty-Four

Harold had told me about Primal Therapy but it took getting used to. At first the crying, sobbing, screaming of other patients overwhelmed me. To find myself dropped into the center of a madhouse scared the hell out of me. Even with rooms closed off, with walls padded, nothing kept heartbroken sobs from seeping into me. The dim, eerie light, frightened faces, took me far from my comfort zone. I felt adrift, scrambled. Did I break barriers down or create new defenses to handle all this chaos? I didn't know.

One of the hardest parts was that I had to be away from our children. I lived alone in Los Angeles for three weeks. During that time, I had therapy six hours a day. I barely ate. I lost weight I couldn't afford to lose. After the first intense period, I had weekly to biweekly sessions lasting hours. What a price to pay for peace. I heard it rare couples stayed married when both went through this ordeal. Harold had started two years before me. He still attended. Sometimes we could share the long drive.

Harold didn't like himself any better than when he started. He became more depressed. What kind of chance was I taking? Would the kids end up with two crippled parents? I risked it.

Lucky for me, I had a talented, sensitive therapist. Bernie stayed calm, seemed to know when to push, when to break things off. He gave me endless time, wouldn't let anyone else work with me. I never screamed. I didn't feel rage. I experienced fear and sadness.

"Bernie, did you feel that earthquake?"

"No earthquake, Karlan. Let yourself roll with what's happening to you. You're safe."

I had strange imaginings of putting my hands around Bernie's throat. He wouldn't fight me but would trust me to do no harm. I didn't know who Bernie became in my mind but felt clean air whip around me. Maybe this could work.

"Bernie, did you feel that earthquake? You had to feel that one. The walls, floor, everything moved. It's going to fall in. Everything's going to fall apart." I felt panic that rolled into a kind of dread. I stayed with it as long as possible. I had no control of when it would stop but I came back into awareness slowly.

After a tedious three-hour session without an earthquake, with nothing happening, I felt strange, disoriented. Bernie suggested I stay in town, sleep at his house with his wife and child.

"I'd like to keep an eye on you. You can have dinner with us, get a good night's sleep, head home in the morning."

"No, I need to get to my family. I'm feeling better, Bernie. But thanks."

I had driven about an hour when a window in my brain seemed to open. I had the strong belief that if I just started swimming, I'd find what I needed. I drove with purpose to Harold's and my favorite beach. Alone in the late night, I stripped to my underwear. My mind promised warmth even though February winds blew. When I stepped in, the waves gentled me, feeling like bath water. I kept swimming, euphoric, excited. I'd find my answers now, I knew it.

I heard my mother calling. Such a loving sound. She beckoned me with a tender voice. The words swam up through my heart into my mind: "Come to me. I'm here, waiting for you."

At some point, I found myself looking down from above. Good heavens, who is that pathetic, freezing woman and what is she doing in the middle of the ocean? Poor thing, she's going to drown. In that instant, my spell vanished. Struggling in the cold water, I could barely see lights on shore. My children would never know I hadn't deliberately killed myself. Harold would anguish forever. More important, I wanted to live. With all my heart, I wanted to live.

# Chapter Sixty-Five

I swam slowly, methodically. Let me live, let me live. Finally I found myself clinging to rocks while being pounded by waves. I heard Harold calling my name. Another hallucination? No. He stood on the beach, a powerful lantern swinging back and forth. I don't remember him getting me out of the water. He had me in the car, wrapped in towels before saying anything.

"You okay?" He moved my face toward him. I searched his eyes, trying to make sense of it. I couldn't talk for a few minutes. Finally my brain went into gear.

"How did you know where to come?"

"I called Bernie when you didn't get home. I figured the beach." He put his hand on my shaking knee. "You're going to be fine. I know a private hospital near here. I visited a patient there. Nothing scary will happen to you . . . just for a few days you'll be given bed rest."

Harold stayed at the hospital with me that night, sleeping in a chair by my bed. I had hypothermia, along with some bruising. I felt lucky. My mind swirled with colors, pictures. Gates in my memory opened. I couldn't close them. Images darted in and out of my mind. I saw those hands coming at me. Instead of being frightened, I studied them: distinctive hands with dirty nails, hardworking hands, hair on the fingers.

I called my mother. "Have we ever known anyone with hands like that? Someone who might have hurt me a long time ago?"

"Absolutely not, Karlan. We always protected you. No one ever touched you."

Two days later, my sister Joan called, her voice subdued.

"I have to tell you something, Karlan. Mother said not to because she's afraid it will hurt you—make you crazy. She thinks you'll forget . . . if we keep still." The line went quiet.

"Joan, I'm not going to forget. If you know anything, sweetheart, tell me, please."

"Okay! Okay, I'm going to Salt Lake next week. Karlan, I have to see your face. I'm changing planes in Las Vegas. Can you meet me at the airport?"

"Can I meet you? Joan, I'll think of nothing else until I see you."

She looked strained as she came out of the airport tunnel. Our first hug felt timid, then we clutched each other like we had as kids. We found a private spot, sat together, our faces inches apart.

"All I know, Karlan, I opened the door in our bathroom in Paris. You had to be about three. The lock didn't hold. I kind of fell in. I saw you on the floor—naked, sitting in blood. Mademoiselle Mallmoray stood over you. You twitched. Your eyes had rolled back." Joan stopped. Tears ran down her cheeks. "I didn't take good care of you."

"Shhh, Joan, you've always taken good care of me. Go on."

"Mademoiselle said not to tell mother. She said you had fits. She wanted to help you. That—the blood just came out of you. God made it come. That's what she said. She told me that if I said anything I'd be going against the will of God. I went to mother as soon as she got home." Joan picked up her small suitcase, put it down, clutched her purse to her chest. "But she wouldn't believe me. 'Mademoiselle Mallmoray loves Karlan.' mother told me. 'She'd never hurt her. God is in this home.'" Joan gave a long sigh.

"What happened after that?"

"Mother went away on one of her trips. She had to have talked to Mademoiselle because our nurse—punished me by putting me in the closet for almost a week."

"Oh, no, Joannie, you hate to be closed in."

"She left the door open. She never acted angry or upset. She seemed like—in a trance. She had everyone in on the punishment: our cook, the housekeeper, even you. I don't know what she told you. No one could look at me. Everyone, even you pretended I didn't exist. All of you walked by me without . . . without seeing me. I cried, I screamed. Nothing did any good. I had a pot in the closet to pee in. Food came on the floor but no one spoke to me the whole time."

"Joan, why didn't you walk out the open door?"

"I never considered it. I must have been terrified of her."

"Where was Hal? He wouldn't go along with any of that."

"At camp, I think. I never said anything again to anyone. I didn't tell Hal, not a soul."

"Did more happen? Did you see anything else?"

Joan got up, walked to the window. I went with her, putting my arm around her waist.

"Do you remember the farm outside of Paris," Joan asked, "where Mademoiselle's cousin lived? We went there a few times."

"I don't remember it. What did the cousin look like?"

"He had dark hair like Mademoiselle, always looked like he needed a bath. I don't know, his clothes smelled." Joan took out a kleenex and wiped her eyes.

"Hal thought he heard you scream. You were in the tool shed with Mademoiselle and her cousin. He saw the cousin carry you out. He asked what happened. Mademoiselle just laughed. 'Oh, she got into chocolate again,' Mademoiselle told him. 'We found her eating it in the tool shed all by herself. It made her so sick. It's happened before. You know, the fits she has.' Later on Hal asked you if you'd been eating chocolate. You told him you had and it made you sick. That satisfied Hal but I think something happened in there. I never told mother."

"Joan, it's not your fault. I'm the one to be sorry for walking by you, ignoring you in the closet. You've suffered just as much as I have. Can you understand mother not checking out what you told her?"

"No, but our mother doesn't want to believe bad things happen . . . to good families. If something ugly did happen, well then it would mean, we weren't living the word of God."

"Joan, I remember hurting when I was little, between my legs. I thought it was something every kid felt, like growing pains. You and mother told me it would go away. How come . . . why didn't she check to see if anything might be wrong?"

"That part, Karlan, I can understand because just like mother, I had to believe nothing happened to you. Otherwise I had, I don't know, to feel guilt. I came to believe it had been a dream. Mother, I guess, couldn't face making such a mistake. Mother and I never talked about it until a week ago. She still wants to believe it didn't happen. I can't explain it better than that."

I rocked Joan in my arms feeling like her big sister.

# *Chapter Sixty-Six*

"You've known all these years, haven't you? Everyone knew but me. All the doctors, you've all known." I didn't feel angry, only disoriented. "Maybe if you told me I had been sexually abused, I would have pieced it together sooner."

"I . . . I wanted to give you the gift of time." Harold sat next to me on our couch, holding my hand. "Even Dr. Rayworth—remember him? You saw him in Provo."

"Of course, I remember Dr. Rayworth but we only talked. How would he know anything?"

"He suspected. He warned me not to overwhelm you, let you remember as you were ready."

"So when we tried to have sex our first night, you weren't surprised?"

"I was shocked. I'm ashamed to tell you what I thought."

"Tell me, Harold, please. I don't want any more secrets."

"I thought your parents knew about the damage. I thought they . . . they wanted to use me . . . blame me. 'The brutal German mutilated our precious daughter, then drove her to insanity.'"

"That is horrible. They wouldn't do that."

"Of course not. I told you, it was crazy." Harold massaged my hand, looking uncomfortable. "That night you . . . you went off the deep end.

I don't blame you, but I felt desperate, frightened. I didn't know if . . . I could handle it."

I put my hand on his cheek. "Thanks for sticking in there. You're a brave warrior."

"You've put up with me."

I shook my head, waved away his balancing sheet.

"That wedding night, mother had to know. That's why she didn't want us to leave. She wanted to put it off one more night. There was a conspiracy of silence, anyway." I could feel anger grip my stomach.

"No, I think she suspected, felt frightened about what might have happened in Paris. Then she panicked when she realized it could come tumbling down."

I sat still feeling heavy.

Harold started talking again but in such a quiet voice I could hardly hear him. "Your father didn't know anything. I feel terrible about that, Karlan." Harold closed his eyes. "I blamed him all these years. His night visits when you were a teenager clouded my thinking. What a horrible judgment." Harold looked miserable.

"Oh my goodness, I helped you establish that direction. I can understand you feeling terrible about it. You, you hate false accusations—judging without . . ."

"I didn't think I could do such a thing to someone else with only flimsy evidence. But I did." Harold held his head. "See, that might have happened to you. You might have grabbed some shred of memory. Suspicion could have grown to a concrete belief. Think about it, Karlan. It would have blocked the truth." Harold spoke slowly. "Could you ever have guessed your nurse and her cousin?"

"No, never. I don't even remember the farmer—just his hands." I let myself feel the weight of it. "I still have more holes than answers but at least I know who. Help me understand my mother."

"She's guilty of not wanting to know, hoping it would go away," he answered. "I understand her better as I've gotten to know her."

"Okay, Harold, explain her to me. I'd like to get rid of this knot in my stomach every time she calls on the phone. She never asks about any of it . . . how my therapy is coming along . . . nothing."

"One thing to remember, Karlan. Your mother had shock therapy and it probably muddled her memories. Half remembered nightmares are the worst kind. You know that."

Harold got up. "I'm going to get some wine and crackers. Do you want cheese?"

"Yes, please."

He took a long time getting things together. I leaned back on the couch. Only two months had passed since my hospital stay. I still felt fragile.

We sipped wine not talking for awhile.

"So explain, please, give me more. Make sense of my mother."

"You told me about her first marriage. You didn't learn about it until when?"

"About sixteen or so. She denied it when I asked her years before. I only learned through someone else."

"That failed marriage had to have been an humiliation for her with a temple divorce, moving in with her parents, two little children in tow." Harold's voice soothed. "The only way she could cope was to pretend it didn't happen. That's why she kept telling Joan she didn't have a first father even though Joan remembered him. It certainly confused Joan but your mother didn't want that to be part of her history. So she erased what she couldn't handle."

"You have so much understanding . . . even love for my mother."

"So do you . . . well, maybe not understanding but love. She's an interesting woman with some major flaws." Harold stopped talking but held up his hand, letting me know he hadn't finished. "I've thought of something else, Karlan. When that first-grade teacher said you were unteachable, your mother wouldn't let you believe that. She read your tea leaves, told you everything would be fine. At that moment in her life, she was in emotional trouble but she still saw you, helped you. In so many ways, your parents have protected you."

I let memories wash over me, all the gentle times I had with my mother and father. The good feelings let me remember something else.

"I miss-spoke a moment ago, Harold, when I called it sexual abuse. Sex never had anything to do with it. I don't know how I understand that but I do. I had cervical damage but not for weird sex. It had something to do with religion. I just don't know what."

"Why do you say that?"

"I remember when I was . . . maybe seven reading the *National Geographic,* well not reading, but looking at the pictures. Young boys were being held down. Something being done to their penises—circumcision maybe or something even worse. The adults looked serious but not cruel or . . . or . . . licking their lips in pleasure. I realized when I saw the pictures I knew about being hurt that way. At the time I didn't think any more about it. I understood then I forgot. I forgot until this morning, when I saw the pictures from the magazine in my mind. I remembered it all, even my moment of enlightenment."

"Are you remembering other things? Don't push it. Let your mind feed you slowly. I don't want to find you in the ocean again."

"I have a pretty strong sense that the big drama is over. I can't stop my mind disgorging, by the way, even if I wanted. I keep seeing the little darning egg Mademoiselle used to mend my socks. She dipped it into wine. Wait, after she dipped it, I drank the wine. Three sips of wine, one bite of chocolate. Lots and lots of wine. The special time was called *'grosscalineau'.* I have no idea what that means. I've asked French speakers. No one has heard of it."

"Is that something you've just remembered?"

"No. I've known that term all my life, no dread associated with it but the special 'grosscalineau' time had the core event."

"Why don't you take a nap, Karlan. You look drained."

"Not yet. I want to own what I remember, what my mind will let me remember. She pushed the wooden egg, the little darning egg, between my legs, softy, delicately. I worried I might pee but nothing else. I don't remember any pain. I never felt afraid of my nurse, just those hands, those dirty, harry hands."

# *Chapter Sixty-Seven*

"You two look shell shocked." This dire observation came from Janet Dunbar. "What you guys need is a king-sized break. And I know just the thing."

Janet and her husband had been facilitators at the Carl Rogers Workshops in San Diego. They believed you could get insight without being pounded silly. Janet didn't think much of Primal Therapy with its aggressive techniques—despite my breakthrough.

"Just go for one weekend. See how you like it. I'll take care of the kids. What do you have to lose?"

Harold didn't look convinced.

"Spouses can't be in the same group?" He kept shaking his head dismissing the whole idea. "I'd consider going if we could attend as a couple."

"Harold, that's the point." Janet sounded frustrated. "Be yourself, not, 'Harold, husband of Karlan,' but just plain, Harold." Janet had her hands on her hips, her large brown eyes sparkling with intensity. "No one needs to find out you're a physician. I'm thinking of you, Harold, most of all. Lose your identity for a weekend. You can find your inner child. Play. Take a risk."

So we went. And my life changed.

When I opened the door to my group, I saw nine strangers . . . and a man whom I felt I had known all my life. I stepped back, feeling confused.

Part of me took in how handsome he was with chiseled features, dark, wavy hair. It looked windblown as if he'd just come in from an early morning run. He sat comfortably in his body. He looked at me with warmth, not the turmoil I felt.

I moved quickly to the opposite end of the room, tried to disappear. This didn't make sense. His warm eyes danced when he looked back at me. I let out a whoosh of air. Get hold of yourself, dummy. What are you, fifteen or something?

Introductions started. I held my breath. He told us his name was Doug. He said more but I couldn't pull it in. My mind raced. Stop this. Behave yourself. I never responded to someone's appearance. Even when I was a teenager, I didn't have movie star crushes. I dug my nails into my arm trying to bring myself back to my senses. My turn came to say who I was but I didn't engage. I sat staring at the floor. When I looked up, all eyes were on me—friendly eyes, waiting for me to introduce myself.

"It couldn't be that bad," smiled the facilitator.

"Sorry, I . . . I went into a thought and got lost."

Good grief, I sounded like a dingbat. Two minutes later, I couldn't remember if I had even said my name. I knew I babbled about having three children and a caring husband. Did I tell them anything about me? This wasn't going well. Damn Janet Dunbar.

When lunch time came, I rushed out of the room, across the grass to the cafeteria. I'd eat alone. I'd get hold of myself. I picked up a tray, pushed it along listening to it rattle on the metal rollers. Everything seemed louder than it should.

The lady putting fruit dishes on crushed ice bent down under the aluminum hood. "Can I help you?" She looked friendly, dressed in pink with a white apron.

Could she help me? I didn't know what I needed. Maybe if I ate, my mind would come back to normal. I'd meditate, that's it. Control first, then I'd figure this out.

People were beginning to stream in. Quick, get through the line. Hide out in a dark corner.

# *Chapter Sixty-Eight*

"You took off like a shot." Doug stood behind me. "Are you that hungry?"

Where did he come from? I stammered an answer. "No, I'm not hungry at all. I'm feeling . . . ." I looked up at him knowing he wouldn't laugh at me.

"You're feeling?"

" . . . confused. That's the best word, I guess."

"Why?"

"My emotions are right on the surface. My usual buffer, well, it vanished. I feel raw."

Doug didn't say anything right away, picked out a salad. "Isn't that the goal?" He sounded relaxed.

"I thought so but it's making me feel, feel off balance."

Silence. Did I want him to go or stay? I wanted him here—next to me. At least I had my self honesty intact.

We stood in the line with our trays. People backed up behind us. The lady in pink pointed us toward the cashier.

"Let's sit over there, Karlan." He motioned to a table off to the side. Good, I must have told the group my name. I walked to our table like a robot. Okay, act natural. Talk to him like you would any stranger. But he wasn't a stranger. It all felt disquieting. We sat down, looked at each other. Both of us began speaking at once. Doug motioned me to go first.

"Ah, well, I wondered, Doug . . . you told the group about your wife—Kristin, is that her name?"

"Yes, Kristin."

"But when you talked about her, you seemed so sad." Damn, that wasn't what I meant to say. I made a value judgment. I sounded pushy.

"That's the way I feel, all right."

"Do you want to talk about her?"

"Sure, why not. Kristin—what to say? She's beautiful, intelligent, creative. I've loved her with all my heart."

"Loved—past tense?"

"Yes, past tense."

We stared at our food. Neither of us felt hungry.

"Is reconciliation possible? You said you had three children." I couldn't seem to stop my mouth. I didn't want to blunder into painful areas. What happened to comments like "interesting group we have" or "read any good books lately?"

"The kids. Yes, the kids." Doug didn't act put off by my bluntness. "But it looks like separation, probably divorce."

"Does Kristin want to try . . . is reconciliation possible?"

"Not really. She feels life has passed her by. She wants more creativity. Besides, she doesn't like me." He said it with a shrug.

I couldn't think how to respond to such vulnerability.

"She doesn't like you, Doug? Hate, now hate, I can understand hate between partners but, 'doesn't like,' sounds poisonous. No passion, no energy. Why are you sticking around?" I could feel myself getting emotionally upset, angry with a woman I had never met.

"The kids. Right now, Karlan, I have no answers. And I'm not expecting anyone to give them to me."

"I don't trust people with answers," I heard myself say.

Doug nodded. He seemed to know what I meant even if my words sounded strange to me.

"By the way," he went on. "I don't agree with Kristin's take on me. I'm likable. What about Harold? Love in the present tense?"

"Yes, emphatically." I felt my heart swell with feelings for Harold. Oh, good, that felt like me, again. I had found my balance. "It's not a conventional marriage, Doug. We battle but we both deeply care. We've come close to divorce. We're stronger now than ever."

"I envy you."

# Chapter Sixty-Nine

When we returned to the group, we went back to our original chairs. I looked around, as if seeing the room for the first time. I saw a cozy, sprawling space with cushions in bright colors, couches and easy chairs along with pictures and two large, healthy plants. What had happened to me when I first walked in? I had seen only Doug. Over lunch he became human. I could manage these feelings. But still, I felt my heart thumping. I hardly knew him. Strike that, I knew this man.

"The dynamics are all wrong here," blurted a pixie redhead. "Why don't you two sit together."

Doug moved to my side. It felt right. What's the redhead's name? Marxie, that's it. Get with the group, Karlan. Who's that older woman over there? What a sour face she has. I think her name is Jane but it doesn't fit her. Jane's a soft name. Our Jane's face must be made of stone. How old? Old, she's old. Over sixty, I'll bet. Why would she come to an encounter group? She looks locked down.

Jane turned toward me. She stared hard, as if she'd heard my thoughts. She started talking, never took her hostile eyes off me.

"I saw a line of people waiting for a workshop." She sounded like a disgruntled school principal. "I didn't have anything to do this weekend so I came in." She said this in a flat tone. Then her voice got harder. "I'll tell you, I'm disappointed. You look like a bunch of whiners. In my day, we accepted our circumstances, made the best of things." She sat back, arms folded, looking pleased with herself.

The facilitator didn't say a word.

The youngest guy in our group had been trying to speak. He'd start then stop. I wanted to hear him. What was his name? I've got to pay attention to names. Such a young, baby face. A cross around his neck, must be religious. Finally he stood up.

I said, "Shhh," I wanted to hear him. I wanted to know why he hurt so much.

"I can't seem to make my way through my loss of faith." He stuttered a little. "Nothing means anything to me. I had all the answers and then they left me. I don't know what to do." He walked behind his chair, leaning into it for support. He had freckles. His skin too red, his eyes a washed out blue. "I was in the seminary when . . . I . . . I've disappointed my family, myself. I want to go to sleep, just go to sleep, can't seem to do it. I want to . . . not wake up." He said that part quietly. If the group hadn't been so still, we wouldn't have heard him. Finally he sat down, tears washing his smooth face.

"That's an outrage." Jane jumped up. "You've been given every advantage. You're not starved. You're not maimed. How dare you think of throwing your life away. You should be ashamed."

Stunned silence. I looked at the facilitator. No help from him. He sat on the couch, not part of the group, just an observer. The divinity student hung his head. I felt powerless. Why? I couldn't get words to come out. I couldn't make sense of the enormous rage I felt toward Jane.

Doug stood up. He spoke quietly but impassioned. His eyes blazed. "Don't judge him. We're not here for that. Listen, keep an open heart."

A collective sigh of relief flowed through the group. Jane sat forward, looking to challenge, then stopped. She fell back into her chair, her arms loose at her side.

# *Chapter Seventy*

That night the group decided on a picnic dinner. No one had an agenda. We had become a cohesive collection of people struggling to be more in tune with our feelings. Jane had turned shy. I noticed the divinity student talking gently with her. I began feeling peaceful, not just with the group but with myself.

As if a bell had sounded, we all stirred to leave, picking up paper plates, crumpled napkins. We headed to our segregated dorms. Doug and I turned right, down a forest path while our group quietly went left. We hadn't spoken of a midnight walk. It happened, felt natural. This small space in time belonged to us. I finally realized Doug felt the same intense attraction. It didn't feel awkward now. We talked about our children. Simple things, our struggles and hopes.

"I learn so much about my kids by listening to their prayers," I told him. "I feel like a hypocrite, though"

"Why's that?"

"Because I'm an agnostic. I'm not sure what or to whom I'm praying but it soothes me."

Doug reflected a moment. "Aren't we all trying to share our feelings?"

"I look forward to it, Doug. But isn't listening to your children's messages to God like reading a kids diary?"

"They know you're there. There's no invasion of privacy."

We walked in comfortable silence. How did this flood of trust happen so fast? I'd give myself this weekend, just two days, nothing more.

Doug told me of his three children. His love for them didn't surprise me but his knowledge of their differences, his understanding of their needs during the unraveling of his marriage, that set him apart.

We turned back at the same moment, both comfortable with what we had found together. Throughout the weekend, Doug and I stayed in the moment. We didn't try to steal away to be together but gave to the group, listening actively. I had never felt so tuned to the voice of others. All of us wished to be better parents, friends and lovers. We needed to be heard, our fears confronted. I liked who I found inside myself.

When the two-and-a-half day session ended, Doug and I took a private moment for closure. We found a grassy spot under a tree. We didn't expect to see each other again.

"I feel a deep richness for knowing you. Thanks for this weekend, Doug."

"I'd like to keep in touch, write to you. What would Harold think of that?"

"I'm sure he'd be fine. He's not possessive."

"I respect your marriage, Karlan. I wouldn't do anything to undermine it."

"I already know that about you."

While we were outside, Harold came to the door to pick me up. When Doug and I returned, the group looked uncomfortable.

"Ah, Karlan, your husband came and, ah, Jane just wanted to help or something. She said you weren't part of the group, hadn't attended. And . . . and that Doug hadn't come either. I'm afraid it sounded like a cover-up." This awkward statement came from the facilitator.

"I didn't mean to cause trouble. It just came out wrong." Jane looked truly upset.

"Don't worry," I said. "I planned to tell Harold all about Doug."

The group looked surprised, a couple of people downright doubtful.

"We're emotionally honest—at least we try to be. That's why we've been married so long."

I gave Doug's hand a squeeze. That was our second real touch since we met. The first happened a moment before. We had held each other, under the trees, our faces gently pressed together. It had been the softest, most intense embrace I could remember. Anyone seeing us would have thought dear friends were saying goodbye. And they would be right.

# *Chapter Seventy-One*

"What was that all about? Harold had a frown but I couldn't tell his mood. He sounded more puzzled.

"I met this guy. Doug's his name. It felt as if we'd know each other in another life." For a few seconds there wasn't a sound. When Harold spoke his tone sounded light-of-heart. "You've been converted in one weekend?" He glanced over at me. "All of sudden you believe in reincarnation? Is that what you're telling me?" He smiled but I also saw some stiffness. He whacked the steering wheel. "You have all the luck. I wanted to meet interesting people. But, oh, no, instead I end up treating an asthmatic."

"Did you have what you needed to treat him?" Damn. I should have empathized. Instead I immediately related to the stressed patient. That always happened. Harold would tell me about a terrible day of emergencies and all my questions would be about the struggling patients—not the tired, sometimes panicked, doctor trying to save their lives. We were quiet for awhile.

"At the last minute I had thrown my medical bag into the car. He needed immediate help so it was a good thing. But what bad luck." Harold turned on the wipers as steadily increasing mist turned the highway to glass. He dropped his speed. Cars whizzed by. The guy behind him honked. "Oh, stuff it, you jerk." He turned to me, talking in a normal voice. "It hasn't rained for a month. The first mist makes for accidents. He'd expect me to treat him if he flipped over on the side of the road."

"And, of course, you would." Why did I say that? Harold looked at me and laughed.

"Always for the victim. Well, sometimes, my sweet, that's me."

"So go on with your story, Harold."

"The asthmatic looked like the picture of health then he started working on his 'mother issues,' Wham, he began to struggle, then, the usual course. If I hadn't been there, he would have gone to the hospital—maybe in real trouble. Once he found 'a doctor in the house', he stayed and risked another episode." Harold flexed his shoulders.

"Stiff? Do you want me to rub your neck?"

"Thanks but not until we get home." He patted my leg. "Back to my asthma patient, we heard all about his controlling mother. Everyone seemed appreciative. Called me a hero and all that crap. I got to learn about everyone else's medical problems as well. I hated it. I'm glad for you—I guess. I would have liked that vacation Janet told me about—you know, where I could forget about being a doctor."

"I'm sorry, sweetheart. I wish that hadn't happened. By the way, I'm not going to see Doug again. He lives here in San Diego. Too hard to maintain a friendship from two hundred and fifty miles."

Harold gave me a startled look. "That's a strange response. You meet someone you feel connected with and you want to let it go? I want to meet this guy. Maybe his wife will like us and we can be a foursome. Invite them for a weekend."

If our invitation surprised Doug, he didn't say so. He came two weekends later. His marriage all but over, Kristin wanted nothing to do with his newfound friend.

Harold kidded me about how clean I made the house, particularly the kitchen.

"If this Doug is such a safe guy, why do you pretend to be someone you're not like a neat housewife?"

"I don't know. Maybe I'm turning over a new leaf. He's coming such a distance, I want him to know I made an effort? Could that be it? I . . . just don't know."

"Don't stress. I'm amused, that's all, but not surprised. I'd want to be my best self with a new friend too."

I could hear Harold and Doug talking while I prepared dinner. I expected light conversation but Harold immediately told Doug about his struggle with depression. I stopped stirring the soup. Harold never told people about that, certainly not a stranger. Then I heard him tell Doug he had been born in Germany. Good Grief! What was going on? Was Doug a sorcerer? That might explain my immediate reaction when I first saw him.

Our three children joined us for supper. After washing up, they came hip hopping to the table where I introduced them to Doug. He stood and reached out his hand. Rick, smoothly, with no awkwardness, embraced Doug with a long hug. Rob and Kendra followed suit. Our kids were affectionate but not demonstrative when meeting a stranger. I hadn't told them much about Doug, only that I had met a nice man at the Carl Roger's workshop. The whole scene had a sense of being a shared past. Harold and I looked at each other a little bewildered.

After dinner, when the kids left for bed, I sat quietly while Harold and Doug talked. They discussed struggling relationships, particularly Doug's efforts to save his marriage.

"Does Kristin want to try therapy? Karlan and I have risked an intense process. It's made a difference. Perhaps the biggest benefit is that we both took such a chance. I don't mean just with our marriage but finding out about ourselves."

"We saw a fine marriage counselor," Doug said. "We both liked him. He told us his purpose wasn't to save our marriage but rather to help us understand what had gone wrong. Then we could decide what to do."

"Did that help?" I asked. That was my first comment since dinner.

"It helped us both but not our marriage. I've tried for several years to be who Kristin wanted. That never works."

Harold flashed me a look. Could he be thinking of how hard he had tried, once-upon-a-time, to make me into someone I didn't want to be? Those days were now ancient history.

Doug didn't notice the look we exchanged. He kept talking. "Kristin leaves the home as she pleases. I've functioned as a single parent. She feels I can't meet her needs. I think she's right."

"So who decided on divorce?" Harold asked.

"Oh, I did. The marriage ended long ago. I need to get on with my life. We're still living in the same house because of the kids. Not a good arrangement."

While I was washing the dishes, Harold came up behind me, wrapped his arms around my waist. He whispered in my ear, "You have great taste in men."

# *Chapter Seventy-Two*

Doug managed a weekend trip about once a month. We seldom went south to visit him. Harold's schedule made that near impossible.

After dinner one evening, our three kids gleefully left to play while I started doing the dishes. Doug jumped up.

"You made the dinner, we'll do dishes."

Harold looked horrified. "We guys don't do dishes."

"Where's that written? And why aren't the children helping? Women aren't maids. What's the matter with you, Karlan, letting this go on?"

I tried to make a joke. Doug wouldn't back down. Harold looked uncomfortable.

"I help sometimes," he said lamely. Doug gave me an incredulous look.

"Well, I see where I can be of use to this family." He gathered the dinner plates. The kids reluctantly helped with Harold watching.

Being a single parent, Doug ran a tight ship with rules both understood and respected. I tried to explain our emotional democracy, full of energy and feeling. At least that's what Harold and I tried to do. Harold's depression plus my anxiety attacks also entered into the mix. Often we had chaos but we kept trying.

I explained this to Doug. He listened carefully but wasn't impressed. Child rearing became an important, never resolved issue between the three of us. I told Doug he seemed too rigid. Harold agreed with me. "I want our kids free of pressure. I want them to feel safe in their home," Harold said.

"Their rooms are disaster areas," countered Doug.

"That's the point," Harold said. "Their rooms belong to them, not us. They can keep them as they please. And their allowance is a right of childhood, not a privilege taken away by controlling parents."

"That's all fine and good, Harold. I'm talking about family cooperation. Children helping, being tuned to the needs of others—not expecting a free ride."

Nothing we talked about diminished the good will the three of us shared. After each trip, Harold and I talked for hours rehashing our conversations with Doug.

"No human being owns another." Harold said with passion. "We don't own our children. We have the responsibility of keeping them safe so they can make their own decisions, not in our image but in theirs."

"Yes, but you and I are messy. Aren't we creating messy adults? Is that in their best interest? I'd like help in keeping the house and yard but I don't want to fight for it."

"Oops, Doug's getting a convert. He's made some good points but he doesn't understand how little free time I have."

"I think he does. He keeps talking about you getting an allergist to help you. He sees how tired you are."

"I noticed Doug paid close attention," Harold said, "when I talked about outside relationships that enhanced who we could be."

"Sure he paid attention to that. You're living that principle. Most husbands would consider my friendship with Doug too risky."

"There is no risk. Did you hear what he said about infidelity in a marriage? Doug couldn't have an affair with you, not after being in our home as a guest. He has a very strong moral code. I knew that the moment

I met him. I was prepared to tell you I didn't feel comfortable if I thought the man you met over a weekend was into a short term romance."

"You like him, don't you?"

"He's stimulating, and, yes, I like him."

# Chapter Seventy-Three

On Doug's next visit, he brought his favorite book, Aldo Leopold's, *A Sand County Almanac*. After Doug left, Harold picked up the book. He thumbed it, started to read a page, went back to the beginning. He didn't put it down the rest of the day. He followed me all over the house reading sections. It felt like old times.

"This is breathtaking, Karlan. Leopold immersed himself in the natural world. I want this in our lives. I want it in our kids' future. What a wonderful gift. Did you give Doug a book?"

"Sure, I gave him what helped me the most in the last few years, *I Never Promised You a Rose Garden*."

Harold's face fell. "That's not comparable. It isn't even that well written. He'll think you have no taste. And why would you stress your problems rather than your strengths?"

"Doug and I are friends. Friends don't pretend with each other. He accepts me as I am. I don't even check my spelling when I write to him. I . . . I wouldn't have been straight, honest with him if I gave him something erudite to impress him."

"You could have given him, *The Secret Life of Plants*. It's one of your favorite books." Harold sat looking at me. I felt uncomfortable, angry with the whole conversation.

"I see Doug as completely grounded," Harold finally said. "He's in his core, true to it without thinking about it. It's his natural state. He's not going to gravitate to the same things that have dominated your life. Don't overwhelm him with psychological intensity."

"If Doug can't accept who I am then so be it. I'm not going to act 'grounded' as you put it if that's not what I feel."

"Wouldn't you like to be more grounded?" Harold's sounded thoughtful not judgmental.

I took a gulp of air, tried to relax, think about the question. "If grounded means knowing what's going to happen inside my head, yes. I want that. If it means acting a certain way to fit in, I'm not interested. I'm thrilled to be finished with the whole episode in Paris. No more hands coming at me."

The phone rang. I took it off the hook. I dialed a number, checked that the line had gone dead.

"What are you doing?"

"I don't want to talk to anyone. I want to finish what I'm saying."

"What if it's a patient? I'm on call, you know."

"Sorry, I forgot. They'll call back."

Harold shook his head.

"By the way, Harold. Why do I still have hallucinations? They aren't frightening any more but they still happen. Usually after I've been at the beach. I can't figure it out?"

"I think you get too much sun when you stay all day. I've been telling you that. Now get back to why you don't want to be grounded."

"I like a lot of what's different about me. The way my mind swims with images, stories, colors. If 'grounded' means giving that up, I don't want it. If it means accepting myself, I'm getting there."

The phone rang. "Styler's Residence," I answered. I listened. "Oh, sorry, we've had some problems with the phone. Dr. Styler's right here." I made a face, handed the receiver to Harold.

A week later, Doug called.

"What did you think of the book I sent you?" I asked.

"I have it right here on the bedside table. I've been trying to get into it but it has so many twists and turns, I don't know who's sane, who's the good or bad. Sorry, I can't seem to connect with it."

My disappointment felt total. What had been at stake about my book? I looked over at Harold who seemed to be studying me. He'd been right again.

Doug paused, changed the subject. "I'm calling to vent. It's about Kristin's parents. We've been close for years. I guess I've been made the villain. I dropped the girls off at their house. They closed the door in my face. I . . . I feel angry. No, more hurt, I guess. I thought we had a relationship beyond, well, I don't know."

"Doug, that's terrible. That's so unfair. What did Kristin say to make them think everything had been your fault? I'm so sorry. You must be miserable." I felt hot with anger.

A long pause filled the line. I waited for Doug to tell me he felt better for my understanding warmth.

"Karlan, I already have a mother. I don't need another one."

He quickly ended our conversation, hung up. I felt sick. I turned to Harold who hadn't stopped watching me since I picked up the phone.

"I don't know how to be a friend. I'm . . . . missing with him." I started crying. "And I so wanted him to understand me better through my special book. It means much more to me then I realized. Maybe . . . maybe if he understood the main character, I wouldn't seem so strange."

Harold gave me a Kleenex.

"He didn't like you treating him like an emotional incompetent."

"I didn't do that. I didn't do anything like that. I hurt because he hurt. Isn't empathy what friends feel for each other?"

"I listened to you, Karlan. You pitied him. He could probably hear you wringing your hands in despair for him." Harold came over to me. He put his arm around my shoulder. "He'll tell you when something feels off. He lets me know when I'm all wet. Boy does he let me know. Saying what he feels is what you admired in him. It's what makes Doug who he is." Harold titled my face toward him. I gave a brief nod.

Doug called that evening. "Sorry about snapping at you. I wanted someone to listen, not feel sorry for me. What I don't like about my reaction is that I dumped my frustration on you."

"It's okay. Harold said I piled pity on you. I can do better." I leaned back on the bed. "Doug, don't ever hold back telling me if I misfire. I may act bruised but it's important that the three of us be emotionally honest together. It's worth the risk."

# Chapter Seventy-Four

It didn't take long for Doug to become a member of our family. His visits turned into celebrations for all of us. Harold let go of his inhibitions. He gave way to fun. Something about Doug's ease let my husband relax.

One Saturday, Harold called out to our three kids: "Doug's coming any minute. What do you say? Would you like a big tub of Kentucky Fried Chicken? We can go to the beach, swim, have fun." Harold ruffled Rob's hair.

The kids looked at each other. Kentucky Fried Chicken? Greasy Kentucky Fried Chicken? What had come over their dad? I could read their faces. I felt the same way.

We played tag football. Kendra couldn't manage it so she threw sand at us. Doug didn't find it cute.

"Cut it out, Kendra. I don't want sand in my eyes."

"Make me." She stuck out her tongue and ran off.

"Ah, Harold, how are we handling 'little princess' when she's a complete brat?"

"Just ignore the bratty behavior. Its hard when we're doing things she can't enter into."

Doug put down the football, walked over to Harold. "You keep making excuses for her and she won't learn to be part of the group."

"Yaaah," chimed in Rob, delighted to have someone put Kendra in her place.

"This is too gorgeous a day to worry about a kid sticking out her tongue. Relax, Doug." Harold hadn't stopped beaming since we arrived at the beach. He ran over to his daughter, tackled her. She squealed.

"Give me an ocean ride, daddy."

"If you promise to stop tormenting Doug."

With Kendra on his shoulders, Harold ran into the surf. I watched Kendra triumphantly survey her kingdom. I didn't care what brought this moment between father and daughter. Joy caught at my heart.

# *Chapter Seventy-Five*

Doug wrote about once a week. His letters were addressed to me. That didn't bother Harold. If he should bring in the mail, he'd call out, "Letter for you—Doug." We often read them together.

One Saturday afternoon Harold came into the kitchen with the just-delivered mail. "Maybe there's something from Doug in this stack. I wish he'd visit . . . ." A long pause made me look up. His face had turned pale.

"What is it?"

Harold opened the letter slowly, carefully, but didn't say a word. He handed me the envelope while silently scanning the contents.

"Remember Dr. Franklin?" Harold spoke quietly as if not wanting to wake up a sleeping family. "He was the researcher who accused me of trying to take credit for his work."

"Oh, I remember him. What is he saying now?"

"This is about him, not from him. It seems he accused another doctor of stealing his work but this new doctor fought back." Harold rubbed his neck. "He proved that Franklin had stolen from him, not the other way around."

"That's wonderful! You've been vindicated. Harold, I'm so relieved." I wrapped my arms around him.

Harold sat heavily on the kitchen chair, dropping all the mail on the table. He seemed to slump into himself. "I have this strange feeling of almost . . . embarrassment."

"I don't understand. Why should you be embarrassed?" I pulled another chair close to him.

"I didn't fight. I gave up and left research with my tail between my legs. I let this miserable, unethical twerp dictate my life. Now this other guy, I don't even know him, he clears my name. Don't you see?"

"Yes, I guess. I remember, though, you were so hurt because your mentor wouldn't listen to you and accused you—hatefully. I didn't blame you for wanting nothing more to do with the department or research." I took his hand. It felt limp.

"You were angry, Karlan. You wanted me to fight. I didn't. I remember feeling guilty even though I was innocent. It was as though defending myself might turn up something about me. It feels like . . . like a shadow lurking, ready to step into the light and expose me."

"Maybe that's what primal therapy has given you, a chance to look at feelings you don't understand." I stood up, gathering the mail. "I'll make some tea. We have a couple of hours before dinner. And the house is so nice and quiet."

Harold held me back. "No, please sit a little longer. I'd like tea but not yet."

I put my elbows on the table waiting for Harold to continue. When he stayed quiet, I finally asked, "Who wrote the letter telling you about Franklin?"

"It's an article with a note from my former mentor. He says how sorry he is . . . 'If I can ever do anything to help you . . .'" Harold shook his head. He made a dismissive grunt. "Anything to help you," he repeated the phrase twice under his breath. "The article," Harold went on, "says that Dr. Franklin has been censured for plagiarism and is no longer associated with Stanford."

"All these years," I said, "so much suffering." I took Harold's hand and kissed his fingers. Then I got up to make the promised tea. We drank it without words.

# Chapter Seventy-Six

One weekend, long after Doug's divorce, he brought a friend whom he had been dating for several months. He had written about her. Harold and I rejoiced because we knew how lonely Doug had been.

"I'm nervous," Harold told me. "What if she doesn't like us."

I shook my head. "From what Doug says, she's very warm, friendly. If Doug loves her, she's going to like us." I felt confident about that. Nothing could ever take Doug away from our family.

I caught my breath when Brenda walked in. She had exotic beauty. I don't know why that startled me. Doug hadn't mentioned her appearance. She looked to be smitten with him. Why not? He was a prize. My stomach crunched into a knot. I forced a smile.

Brenda sat on the couch between Doug and Harold. Her wavy dark hair kept falling over her eyes when she leaned toward one and then the other. She leaned toward them a lot. I watched and couldn't make myself move. When she turned toward Harold, she gave him her total attention. Harold looked pleased.

I watched them. I didn't know what to do with my hands. I felt awkward, uncomfortable in my own living room. I should make dinner. That's what I should do. At least I knew how to cook.

Two hours later, Brenda couldn't say enough about what a great dinner I had made.

"Doug told me you were a marvel in the kitchen," she gushed. "He certainly didn't exaggerate. Lucky Harold." Brenda had a dazzling smile, such even, perfect teeth.

It didn't surprise me when she asked Harold to take a walk with her. This left me alone with Doug to do the clean up. For once he didn't press the boys to help. He kept watching me out of the corner of his eye.

Finally, I said something. "She's beautiful, Doug, and seems head-over-heels in love with you. I'm glad for you." I smiled up at him.

"What else do you think?" Doug stopped washing and looked right at me. "About Brenda, I mean."

"I can't tell. I don't know her. Give me time."

"How can you get to know her if you hide. You're acting very strange."

Harold and Brenda came back from their walk. Brenda looked pleased. Harold looked in shock. Not until we went to bed that night did I find out why.

"Good God, Karlan, she . . . she expected me to be 'on her side.' That's what she said, 'on her side.' She's jealous. She thought I'd be waiting for my chance to get Doug out of our lives. Can you imagine? I love Doug, too. 'He's a family friend,' I told her." Harold looked at me waiting for a response. I only wanted to listen.

Finally I took a long breath. "I learned something about me today. And I don't like it. I felt left out and the feeling hurt like hell." I pulled on my hair. "I thought myself a true friend but this afternoon, I was a petty, jealous child." Harold took my hand away from my hair but he didn't say anything. "What I wondered, what I've been thinking about, do you have those same feelings? I mean, the ones about being left out . . . when Doug and I have long conversations or take walks alone. You encourage us but don't you feel jealous?"

"I've had all kinds of feelings since Doug came into our lives. But the basic, core response is that I ended up having the very friend I wanted when I went to that Carl Roger's Workshop. You happened to bring him into our family but he's nourished me as well." Harold pulled me to him. "And another thing, I like who I've become by working through those feelings. I've also seen you flourish. That matters to me."

"Well, you're way ahead of me, then. I found out I wanted all your attention and Doug's as well. I want to be enough for both of you, be primary to two men. I don't want to share with anyone."

Harold laughed. "You certainly know how to dig out the worst possible interpretation of your feelings. You're nothing like that. Your good antenna picked up how wrong Brenda would be for Doug. If a lovely, warmhearted lady had walked in, you would have celebrated." Harold kissed me gently. "Trust Doug, I think it was Brenda he learned about on this trip—not you."

Doug never did like to be smothered. Brenda dropped out of the picture. There were others over the years but none serious enough to warrant a visit to Santa Barbara.

# *Chapter Seventy-Seven*

At forty-eight, Harold entered a gray world. The gloomier he felt, the harder to find pleasure in anything. Food tasted like straw, music had no sound, his body didn't respond to touch.

"Karlan, it isn't anything you're doing. I know I've blamed you in the past. I think I believed if you just achieved everything I knew you capable off, I'd be well." I smiled at him. Now I knew he was feeling better. It sounded like my Harold again. For a week he'd been so low, I didn't see how he managed to practice medicine.

"None of this is your fault." Harold kept massaging my hand. He did that when he had an important point to make. Trouble was, my joints hurt. I felt loath to pull away. His touch came rarely these days. "You're an exciting lover, a good cook. I just can't taste or feel. It's all about neurotransmitters. Mine are fouled up. I'm going to get through this. Don't give up on me."

"Tell me how to help. Don't close me out. When you come home, sit in the car staring into space for an hour, I feel helpless. Come in or if you want, I'll come out. Let's be a team with this."

On black days, I couldn't reach Harold. What energy he had, he gave to his patients. I checked with his nurse, Sharon.

"His sense of humor is asleep," she said. "But he comes across as thoughtful, caring just as always. He's much slower, sees about a third less patients. I try to take care of the small stuff."

"Thanks Sharon. How about the other doctors? Is there flack about his not producing?"

"A few are grumbling. He needs to stop working at the free clinic in L.A. He can't donate time when he's . . . ."

"Of course, I'll talk to him about that. He seems to gets so much pleasure when he's working free. I don't know what that's about. Let me know if something comes up you think I should hear about."

"Sure. And, Karlan . . . Harold said you're having swollen joints again. Do you think that comes from stress? I mean you're worrying about him all the time."

"I don't know what's going on with me. Right now, headaches bother me more than my joints. Harold gave me a big dose of prednisone. That took care of it until the next time. I guess I have rheumatoid arthritis. Not a diagnosis I'm happy about. And why should that give me headaches?"

"Are you seeing any other doctor except Harold?"

"Sharon, I've seen everyone you can possibly imagine, physicians, chiropractors, acupuncture's. I've been given so many different diagnoses . . . . including 'hysteria.' One doctor told me I couldn't understand the concept of, 'psychosomatic,' without going to medical school. Sometimes I'm fine, then, all of a sudden, I can't move. Harold and I are a pair."

Doug didn't travel to Santa Barbara when Harold entered deep depression. He didn't come if my joints made movement difficult. We kept track of each other with letters. When he did come, the whole family rejoiced. It felt like a homecoming.

One trip was memorable. Harold had picked up the phone when Doug called. The sound of our friend's voice made Harold plead for a visit.

When Doug arrived, Harold tried to participate. He came to the table in his brown velvet evening jacket with a colorful scarf at his neck. He even tried to force a smile. I had cooked a celebratory dinner. But my heart sank when I saw Harold. He looked worse than he had a few hours earlier. He sat staring at his plate, never lifted his head, never took a bite. A gray gloom fell over the table. None of us spoke. The boys managed to eat. They had become used to his misery. Kendra tried to take her father's hand. He didn't notice. Doug and I looked at each other in equal pain. As soon as Harold left the table, Doug gathered his belongings to return home.

"He doesn't need me now," Doug said. "He needs only you."

# Chapter Seventy-Eight

I gave thanks to the old lady who had once owned our home. I learned she had recently died at the age of eighty-six. I had always planned to write her a letter of gratitude. Not only did she love flowers but had whimsy in her planting. I imagined her in a big apron, pockets full of seeds, walking through our acre of land while she sang and scattered her treasure. Most of the blooms lay hidden under the tall weeds I had neglected all summer. Other must have been blown against rocks where they found a bit of soil and flourished. I never planted seeds. I put in bulbs and nursery plants. It was her efforts that took my breath away on this September morning. Cosmos with their daisy like flowers blew gently. Gloriosa daisies made a carpet of gold competing with orange and yellow marigolds. All of them should have died out years ago. The old woman's nurturing spirit must be alive in my garden.

I stepped on the porch. No one was awake. Just me. I let myself embrace hope for the first time in months. For two mornings in a row, Harold had emerged from our bedroom with a smile. He sounded like himself. He ruffled Rob's hair. He asked Rick about basketball and listened attentively while our son described his whole game. He pulled Kendra on his lap calling her his princess. He asked how my joints were doing while giving me a hug. My eyes embraced our garden. I felt blessed, I believed in tomorrow.

A few hours later, I found Harold on his stationary bike. He was lathered in sweat, listening to a medical tape. Then I noticed a book propped up in front of him. That I hadn't seen before, three things going on at once. He took off the earphones.

"I'm reading Greek poetry. I like looking back. Things aren't that different through the ages." He looked excited, like a kid winning his first race.

I started to respond but stopped when I looked into his eyes. They seemed too bright. Froth bubbled at the edges of his mouth.

"Harold, you're overdoing. Try meditating. I'm concerned your . . . ."

"No, you don't understand, Karlan. This is something wonderful. My mind is zinging. I could do ten things at once. I can hardly wait to get to the office. I'm going to book more patients. My colleagues will love me." His smile blossomed into a throaty laugh. "Oh, how they'll love me."

My mind flew back to Harold's frenetic energy in medical school. I had been excited for him then. Not now. I felt an ominous ache in my stomach. I hated to see him imprisoned by depression but this . . . this kind of wild energy, felt almost insane.

On Thursday Harold went to the clinic early. I waited a few of hours before calling Sharon.

"He's fine, Karlan," she reassured me. "Full of energy. He's already seen four patients and they were beaming as they left the office."

I put down the phone and tried to quiet my fear.

The next morning Harold didn't jump out of bed as he had the day before. I took a deep, grateful breath. Okay, he's back to an even keel. For the first time in twenty-four hours, I let myself relax.

With the house quiet, the kids off to school, I went to my sanctuary—the garden.

Harold joined me shortly afterwards. He looked radiant.

"Something amazing is happening, Karlan. I finally understand your world. I'm living with my complete brain for the first time—all parts of it."

I dropped my pruning shears. I felt like I did when one of our children came too close to the edge of a cliff. My innards recoiled. Fear grabbed my heart. I knew immediately, Harold had gone into a frightening, different world. His speech sped faster and faster.

"There's this glorious silver fish right in front of me. She knows everything. She's telling me what I've never understood. Now I can help my patients. All these years I've been working with one hand tied behind my back, scrambling, trying, failing. Always failing. No more, no more." He marched in a halting, twisting circle around me. He wouldn't look at me. I needed eye contact. I had to reach him.

"Harold, darling, this isn't enlightenment. You're hallucinating. You're . . . you're manic. You understand that state of mind. You've explained it to me. This is the time to get help."

Harold backed away from me shaking his head violently. I reached for him but he jerked away. I gave him space, kept my voice calm.

"Remember all those times you helped me? Remember when I nearly drowned? If I had stayed with that hallucination, I'd be dead."

His face turned rageful, ugly. "Don't try to take this away from me, Karlan. I've starved my whole life. You've, you've had it all. You want to keep me with just half a brain. I want my chance in paradise too."

"I'll call Jim. This is when you need your therapist. Trust me on this, Harold. I'm on your side. I don't want to take anything healthy away from you."

He quickly closed the space between us but he looked over my head at something above me. "Hell, no. I don't need help. For the first time in my life, I can . . . I can finally give my best to my patients, my kids, to everyone."

I followed him to the car, quietly begging him to come in, call his psychiatrist. He kept shaking his head, breathing like he'd run an uphill race.

"Where are you going, Harold? I don't think you should drive."

"I'm going to the clinic, of course. I've never in my life been more alert or better able to drive." He slammed the door, sped off.

For ten seconds I stood frozen. Then I called Sharon. "Cancel his patients. He shouldn't . . . he mustn't practice medicine. He'll argue. Don't let him convince you. Tell him it's my decision. I'm calling his therapist." I gave a long anguished sigh. "I'm also calling the head of the clinic."

I left a message for Jim. I knew he couldn't get right back to me. He'd be with a patient at this hour. My hand shook when I dialed the number for the physician in charge of the clinic. His response took me aback.

"Do you know what you've just done? By law, I have to stop him from practicing medicine. Are you qualified to make a decision that could ruin his career?"

"If Harold drove a truck or flew planes," I answered, "I'd stop him. He doesn't understand his limitation. He thinks he's God." I bit down hard on my teeth to keep my sobs under control. "I love him too much to let him destroy himself, make a wrong decision. Can't you understand that?"

"I can understand what I'd think if my wife did this to me. Only a psychiatrist should be calling me. Not you."

About an hour later, Harold came in the door.

"You did it. You had me locked out of my office."

"I had to, Harold."

"Is that right? Just leave me alone, Karlan. Let me make some choices on my own." He locked himself in our bedroom.

I paced, sick with worry, second guessing, not knowing what to do. When he came out an hour later, he looked beaten. His glow had turned to a gray pallor.

"I'm going to see Jim." He stopped, looked at me. "I don't know what you said to him but . . . . I don't know when I'll be back."

"Could I drive you, come with you?"

"No!"

Two hours later, Jim called me.

"First of all, he knew you would stop him. He wanted your good sense to protect him. You didn't let him down."

"What's going to happen?"

"I'm going to be in charge for awhile. I've talked to the clinic. He's going to be on sabbatical leave. No more self-medicating." The line stayed quiet for a few seconds. I knew Jim was still there. I waited, feeling his next words would be crucial. "Karlan, see this for what it is: a breakthrough that will save his life."

I went out to my garden, fell on my knees and wept.

# Chapter Seventy-Nine

Harold staggered toward me, clutching his chest. "Get me . . . ." I could barely hear him. He groaned through clenched teeth. "Get me to the hospital."

I drove fast, the tires screeching into the emergency parking lot.

"Heart attack," someone in a white coat whispered as they placed Harold on a gurney,

For a moment I stood alone in the parking lot, not wanting to go in, not wanting to hear the worst. I needed to hide in the blackness of the night—just for a moment.

It was quiet in the cubical where two doctors worked on Harold. Then I heard him give an agonizing yell. I slipped through the curtains, ignoring a nurse who tried to hold me back. I looked hard at Harold. He finally felt my eyes and turned to me.

"You're getting help," I said. "Know you'll be okay. Trust them." My voiced sounded calm, soothing. It surprised me. I didn't know where such assurance came from.

Harold relaxed. He managed a long breath. A nurse came with a little bottle of pills. The physician nodded. She slipped one under Harold's tongue. Within seconds, his pain ended.

"I don't know what's going on," the cardiologist told me. "I don't think he had a heart attack. We'll do more tests tomorrow."

I blinked trying to see the doctor who had been a guest in our home only six months ago. He had looked so different then, just another guy like Harold. Now he became godlike, pronouncing oracles that could change our lives.

"Tonight he needs to be in his own bed—with you, Karlan." The doctor gave my shoulder a gentle squeeze. "You and nitroglycerin are the best medicine."

When we got home, I helped Harold get undressed. He moved like a rag doll, then fell instantly to sleep.

Not me. I stared at our arched, wooden ceiling. Just the night before, I had studied the wood patterns and made out scenes of rolling hills and gentle streams. Now the same patterns became menacing faces with screaming mouths.

Only a few months had passed since Harold's manic attack. He had made monumental progress, We had been talking about trying a game of tennis. We had looked for a movie to see with the kids. We had been pulling the pieces together to make a family again. I couldn't accept this new crisis. And it seemed worse that the doctors didn't know what was going on.

An angiocardiogram showed a narrowed artery in Harold's heart. The surgeon said it was a cholesterol buildup which limited blood flow.

"No way," I argued, "his diet is pure, he couldn't have a problem like that."

"Heredity can do it."

I felt unreasonable rage. The doctors could talk circles around me.

The spasms kept coming. Harold's eyes would grow large with fear as he struggled to get nitro under his tongue. He always carried three pills in a little paper envelope in his pocket during the day, another three under his pillow at night.

Something about warm water helped him. He felt safe in our hot tub so soaked there several times a day.

"I've never had a spasm if I'm warm," he said. He looked like a content frog in a witches pot with the bubbles popping all around him

"We have to fix that artery," said the cardiologist. "You need open heart surgery.

"No, no, I don't want any part of that," Harold jumped like he had been rammed by a cattle prod. "I don't want to risk being opened up. I'd rather live with the nitro and our hot tub."

"It may not continue to work so effectively," another doctor broke in.

The uncertainty seemed as bad as his depression. I watched for signs of that monster's return.

Everything focused on Harold. The children stayed quiet. None of their friends came to visit. I had long since given up my evening classes, the League of Women Voters and my book club with cherished friends. We didn't see anyone. We didn't go out.

Harold played classical music and read everything he could find about angina. He went through old family records and learned that several young men, distant cousins, had suddenly died without warning. It appeared to be a heart attack but they had never been diagnosed with heart disease. Could this be an inherited problem? At least Harold had a quest, a focus. I had nowhere to go with my energies. I didn't want to leave him alone in case he couldn't get to his nitro. My garden saved me. The months rolled slowly by, converged, folded in on themselves. Time felt meaningless.

One Monday morning Harold called me from the porch. I answered, "Coming."

He didn't wait but hurried to the mulch pile I had been aerating. He looked more excited than I had seen him in ages.

"I have to show you something. Come on in." He hurried off looking back to make sure I followed. I couldn't help but feel his excitement.

I washed my hands and joined him in the living room.

"There's this new procedure, Karlan." He patted the seat next to him. After I sat down he took my hand. "I think it's the answer. It isn't much more traumatic than having angiocardiography and I've done that."

"What is it? Did George tell you about it?"

"No, I just called him. He heard of it but thought it too experimental. He didn't want to get my hopes up but it sounds good to me."

"So tell me. What is it?"

"It's called balloon angioplasty. What they do is insert a catheter with a little bulb at the end. When the right spot is found in the artery, the bulb is inflated. It's ingenious! The cholesterol is flattened. No more pain, no more nitro. We can be normal again."

His doctors didn't agree.

"It's too soon, Harold. Give the procedure another year to get the kinks out."

"I don't want to wait," Harold said. "I'm tired of living like this. I'm afraid to do anything that might trigger an attack. Who wants to live in a hot tub for a year? I want to live now."

He told me this on our drive home after the consultation. I didn't say anything to Harold but their misgivings made sense to me.

"We've been homebound for too long," he went on. "What do you want to do? How can we celebrate life?"

I hadn't thought about what I wanted for months. I felt giddy with expectation.

"Let's take a weekend trip to Palm Springs. I could hear enthusiasm in my voice. "You feel good there, it's warm and the kids love it."

"Maybe." He looked doubtful.

I know," he said. "Let's get Doug to come for a visit. We always have a great time. The kids will like that better than Palm Springs."

"I think he's in Tahoe at his family cabin, I answered. "I haven't even written to him in a couple of months."

Doug responded to our invitation by return mail. "How about fourteen days from now?" he wrote.

But the celebration weekend with Doug didn't happen. The San Francisco specialist called as soon as he received Harold's letter. The months Harold thought he would have to wait to be treated, disappeared.

"You're just the candidate we wanted for our new procedure. If you can get here in a week, we'll be able to send you home a new man within a couple of days."

Harold was as excited as a child having a birthday party for the first time. He had his bag packed before even consulting his physicians. No one could stop him now.

I canceled Doug's visit. We sent Kendra to her loving baby-sitters. The boys went to friends. We would be gone only three days.

# *Chapter Eighty*

We arrived in San Francisco in high spirits. The hospital rolled out the red carpet. Harold was to be the star attraction at a cardiology conference. From beginning to end, his balloon angioplasty would be filmed then shown at the meeting. I imagined Harold stepping off the operating table and waving to the doctors as the credits rolled by.

"What I can tell the physicians," said the cardiologist, "is that we have a doctor in so much pain he can't practice medicine. Then within a few hours, he is free of that pain. The next day he's on a plane home to a new life."

"Oh, does that sound good." Harold let out a long sigh. "I'm sick of waiting for the next spasm. Anticipating the damn thing is almost as bad as the actual seizure."

"We're going to be overly cautious with you, Harold. This won't be done in a lab but in our cardiac surgery theater. If anything should happen one of the top surgeons in the country will be right there to step in."

The cardiologist beamed. I felt his energy, his excitement. He loved his craft, cherished making a difference. Harold would be safe in his hands.

The next morning I waited in a quiet, little room. I brought a good mystery along but the doctor told me I'd barely get into the plot before it was time to see Harold.

"We'll be done in two hours and you can see him right away."

I started getting nervous when three hours passed. No news. A friendly volunteer said she'd track down the delay.

"Probably an emergency came in," she said. "That's what usually happens when things get backed-up." She returned pink-cheeked, cheerful. "I had it right. A heart attack patient took your husband's operating room. Don't know why you weren't told."

I tried to push away the tight feeling in my gut. Don't be silly. If any thing had gone wrong, they'd tell you by now.

I didn't recognize Harold's cardiologist when he walked into the waiting room. He looked years older. Two other men in white stood on either side of him as if to give support.

"Karlan, stay calm," he told me. "First of all, he's alive. He's a fighter . . . and . . . we're doing everything we can."

I had stood to greet them. Now I fell back in my chair. "Wait a minute, wait a minute. What happened? Where is he?"

The older doctor, tall and stiff, looked down at me. I couldn't see beyond his frown.

"We've just done open-heart surgery. We have a high success rate at this hospital. Best in all of San Francisco but because this was done in a lab, not our surgery theater, we . . . ."

"My God. No. Not in a lab."

The cardiologist took my arm. I felt his hand shake. "An emergency. We didn't have the surgery theater available. No other time before tomorrow's presentation. Harold agreed to do it in the lab."

"Not me. I didn't agree." I struggled not to cry. A beeping sound came from the surgeon's pocket. All three rushed out.

I fled to the bathroom. My gut turned to water. Cramps kept coming telling me over and over, a terrible thing has happened, a terrible thing has happened. I felt weak, helpless. Finally I curled on the floor holding on to myself. Someone stood by the stall. She didn't go away. I watched her shoes. They were white. She stood absolutely still, waiting, waiting. I got up, came out of the stall. The nurse led me to the sink. I washed my face, my hands all the way up to my elbows. Maybe I could wash it all away. She handed me a white smock and a net for my hair. Finally, she spoke.

"Hold on," she said.

I made my eyes focus on her. She looked upset. No, no she looked angry. Her protective face-mask dangled around her neck. She had tons of freckles, red hair streaked with gray. I saw laugh lines but now her face looked grim.

"Come on." She took my arm. Did she tell me her name? I don't remember. Her shoes, quiet on the smooth floor, felt grounded. I watched her face. She had power. If she would only say the right words, Harold would be . . . Harold would be safe.

"This is going to be the worse thing you've ever seen. I took care of your husband before he went for his procedure. I know the shock you're going to have." She stopped, looked at me. She wanted to hug me. I could tell but she held back. She took a long breath and went on. "A little while ago, he opened his eyes. He asked for you. The doctors wanted . . . to wait . . . until he looks better. But he needs you now."

I saw a large room, lots of windows. It felt like a white castle. Harold lay on a gurney, completely naked except for long tight socks. His skin drained of color. What was that under him? Finally I got it. He lay in a pool of congealed blood, his blood. Hoses coiled in mounds went into different parts of him. The machinery, large, living, like obedient giants, spoke in peeps and gurgles. Lots of doctors, nurses. They moved through the maze with grace. I thought them dancers on a stage.

"What the hell is she doing here? Get her out, now!" Gruff, ugly voice. Who said it? I couldn't tell, all wore masks. I stood rooted, stared. I blinked to clear tears I didn't know had fallen. Harold. His trussed up chest didn't seem to belong to him. The angry rip overtook his body. Another huge gash ran from his hip to his knee. I tried to find reality, some connection to what I knew. I couldn't flounder. I'd stay grounded, a witness to this—carnage.

Harold opened his eyes, looked right at me. His voice sounded like the voice I knew, clear, young.

"I've become a fighter, Karlan. I'll, . . . I'll . . . I love you, I love you." His words a gift, death at his elbow.

# *Chapter Eighty-One*

"He's stronger," a new nurse told me the next morning. She reached for my hand and led me to an elevator.

I had spent the night in a daze. I don't remember anyone putting me into the cold, stark-white hospital room. Pills I never took, water I never drank, seemed to stare at me, mock me. I sat on a wooden chair rocking back and forth afraid to rest. If I gave into comfort, Harold might slip away.

"He's stronger," she said again. The words didn't seem real. Then I saw him. Cleaned, draped in white. He looked terrible, worse then yesterday. I tried to gently put my arms around him. I needed to hold him safe, push reality away. His eyes opened. He looked startled.

"You—you're here." He almost smiled. "I need to, to hang in there so my body can recover. Please don't leave again. I can't do it without you."

"Where would I go? You're my center, my focus."

I made arrangements for the children to fly up on the weekend. I talked calmly to Rick but he heard.

"You're frightened, mom. I can tell by your voice. Is he going to die?"

"I don't know." Not what I meant to say.

I tried to prepare the kids before I brought them to Harold's room. No matter what I said, it would be a shock. Kendra ran in, hugged him. Then she saw him. Her hands slipped to her side. She curled on the floor like I had in the bathroom

"We're here dad. We'll make you strong. Don't leave us." Rob said this, his face tight. He bit his lip.

"Oh, my darling, my darlings. I've been away so long. It seems like years. I'm so glad you're here." Harold rocked his head back and forth. Was he in too much pain? He kept talking. He seemed . . . agitated, twisting under the sheets, twisting despite his wounds.

"My mind is telling me things. Things I don't want to think about," he murmured more to himself.

"Shhh," I told him. "You need all your strength. This isn't the time to go back."

"I can't. I can't stop it."

I started for the door. He should be sedated. "I'll get help, sweetheart. Hold on."

"Karlan, stop." He tried to pull himself up. "Stay here, please. Stay beside me."

"Okay, Harold. Okay. You're in charge."

"Need to tell . . . ." He let go of the bed railing. "It's always been there, just under the surface. I couldn't pull it out. Wanted to . . . to remember." After each phrase there were long pauses. He seemed to sleep a few moments then gather the energy to go on.

His eyes darted open again as if no time had passed. "An officer . . . he looked so sad, so sad . . . said we lost the war. 'No more blood,' he said."

Kendra looked frightened. She moved over to a chair, curled up. I turned on the television without sound. A cartoon held her eyes. The boys stayed by their father, holding on to him.

"It happened at the end of the war. Remember? I might have told you. I tried to blow up a German ammunition dump?"

I nodded. The boys knew the story too.

"How old were you, dad?" Rob whispered the question in his ear.

Harold stayed still for several seconds. He looked intently at Rob.

"I was your age, son—fourteen."

"Go on, dad, go on." Rick smoothed his father's hair, caressed his cheek.

Harold started again. "Something happened first. We ran, Karl and I . . . Did I tell you about Karl?"

I shook my head.

"We ran—after our officer told us to scatter. 'Get away,' he said, 'get away from this madness.' We all ran."

Harold fell back to sleep. His breathing steady. No more twitching. Then his eyes flew open.

"Patrols! Kids like us. Tracking down the deserters. Karl . . . He went one way. I dove into the brush. They caught Karl."

"Oh, dad, what happened?" One of the boys said it. I kept focused on Harold. His eyes looked huge in his shrunken face.

"Pushed him, bunch of boys, just boys. An officer . . . older. Good . . . good, he'll stop them, stop the bullying. Karl so gentle, so beautiful."

Harold closed his eyes, said words that didn't make sense. Maybe he was speaking in German. Both boys stroked him. I stood at the end of the bed, watching. I wanted this demon gone.

"Say it, Harold. Be done with it," I whispered.

"Karl never looked my way. He called out, something about his father. And then . . . they put a rope around his neck, slung one end to a branch." Harold words became strong, clear. "I watched my best friend hanged. But I didn't make a sound."

None of us moved. We held our breath.

"That's when I decided to destroy . . . to blow . . . up something. To make the war end. I forgot about Karl. All this time, I forgot."

# *Chapter Eighty-Two*

Harold made slow steady progress for a month. I believed his reawakened memory made the difference. I saw peace in his face, peace that would let his body heal.

Then it all went sour.

The infection started in his thigh spreading to the rest of his body. He fought, day after agonizing day.

Two of Harold's colleagues from Santa Barbara came to check on him. We had lunch together. They seemed ill at ease, hesitant.

George put down his napkin. "Harold's cardiologist never read his medical records."

He stopped, looked at me. His voice became quieter. "Because the surgery was an emergency, doctors didn't have time to scrub properly. Of course, massive infections were probable."

It was a medical nightmare," Mark added. "He didn't have a cholesterol buildup. He had a congenitally narrowed artery. Under stress, it fibrillated."

"A balloon angioplasty was the last thing he should have had." George shook his head. "Caution would have been the order of the day for a new procedure like this but . . . sometimes doctors skip over what they consider bothersome procedures when it comes to treating a fellow physician. That's what happened to Harold."

"Does Harold know about this?"

"Yes. He told us to tell you—calmly. The thing is, it was all preventable. The lab work done here showed low cholesterol readings but no one looked at the results before doing the procedure."

Two weeks later, the cardiologist and his assistant bounced into Harold's room.

"Ah, our favorite patient," said the specialist. "Good news, your fever has broken."

"You can go home tomorrow or even today," chirped the other doctor.

We could only stare. They didn't wait for our response. The doctors turned on their heals and left.

"What do we do now?" I looked at Harold's incredulous face. "You're not well enough to travel."

"They know that." He spoke without bitterness. "There's so much organ damage, I'm just staying alive because I started out with a strong body. When I die at home, they'll feel off the hook. Let's go, kid. Last chapter, I get to choose. And I want to be in my own bed."

An airline strike meant we had to return home by train. It seemed too strenuous. Harold said it would be fun. "I always wanted to go first class by rail. Never could afford it. Now's our chance."

He asked me to get a bunch of twenty dollar bills. I couldn't think why and I didn't want to tell him three hundred dollars would empty our bank account. If he didn't have some funds hidden away, we were flat broke. I had maxed out our credit cards on the expensive train tickets.

Harold had a benevolent look on his ashen face as he handed out twenties to all the train people who helped him. One old porter spoke up.

"Sir, no need to do that. We all be brothers. We be helping you now."

As soon as we had settled in our comfortable seats, Harold turned to me more alert than he had been for days.

"Karlan, there's a lot we have to talk about. I wish we didn't need to . . . to spend these last moments this way. But I have to explain."

I wanted to tell him to save his strength, to sleep. But he seemed determined. I sat still, my hands folded on my lap.

"I don't want you to sue." He leaned forward his voice full of passion. "I know . . . I know, lots of mistakes were made and it would be quickly settled out of court."

"This is what you want to talk about? No! Concentrate on getting well."

"Please, listen to me, Karlan. I need you to promise me. I don't . . . want . . . you . . . to sue."

"So how does that help other patients? The same mistakes will keep happening. Those doctors were arrogant, made promises, tried to cover up their mistakes. They didn't practice good medicine."

"I agree with everything you're saying. My point is that balloon angioplasty is going to save lives. If you sue, it will slow down the research. Someone who has a cholesterol buildup, might die from the delay." Harold closed his eyes. He didn't go to sleep. His hands kept moving, clenching, stretching

I watched fields pass by, saw children waving. I remembered waving when I was little, wondering who the important people were on the special pullman cars. I couldn't make myself wave back.

Harold's voice broke in. "This is important to me. I don't want my legacy in medicine to be a lawsuit. They are all men of good will. Sure, they're flawed—just like me."

"Okay," I said quietly.

"Another unpleasant subject. I've given people money, a lot of money."

"What kind of money? Who did you give it to?"

"I helped out patients at the free clinic. It's done now. I didn't spend it on myself or gambling or something foolish. Each time I gave an envelope full of cash I thought that person's need was greater than mine, or yours or even the children. I'm so sorry. I believed I would have years to make everything right. I'm sorry. I'm leaving you with an empty financial nest."

# Chapter Eighty-Three

We arrived at our driveway to a huge sign: "WELCOME HOME DAD." The three kids jumped up and down. Harold pulled himself out of the car trying to hug all three at once. Then he stood, gaping at his surroundings, as if he'd never seen such beauty. I ran to help him but he put up his hand.

"Let me take it in." He held on to the car door. I don't want to move for a moment." He looked weak but at the same time, beautiful. "My cup runnith over." His tears seemed to wash away all he had been through.

Rick and Rob got on either side of their father, helping him into the house. Harold had found new energy.

"You know what I feel like?" he said. "Chinese. I want lots of tastes. Rick will you get a little of everything?"

I looked in my purse that held only loose change.

"This one's on me." Rick smiled with a new look of maturity.

Harold walked slowly to his desk, sat down heavily. He put his head in his hands and slept. When he finally looked up, piles of bills, personal letters, medical journals, faced him. He brushed them aside. Then he saw a banded stack of letters from Doug.

"Why didn't he write to the hospital?"

"I never told him." I wandered around the living room distractedly. Finally, I turned back to Harold. "I didn't think of anyone but you. I had tunnel vision, I guess." I picked up a letter, then put it down. "I don't know what to tell you, Harold. What little attention I had left went to the kids." I went over to him, put my hand on his shoulder. "And they didn't get much." This brought tears to my eyes. It felt good to be connected enough to cry.

"How did you take care of the house expenses?"

"I didn't. I never thought about it." I shrugged. "You always paid everything. It didn't seem important."

"Good Lord," he tried to stand up. "I'm surprised the lights are on."

Rick returned with our Chinese feast just in time to hear Harold's last comment.

"Everything's okay. I called the utility companies, told them our situation. They gave us an extension. Lucky you've got such good credit, dad."

Rick put out eight small containers filled with Chinese delicacies. Harold started eating as if starved. After two bites he stopped. His face turned white. He looked at us with a soft, resigned smile.

Kendra sat looking at her food.

"Aren't you hungry, Princess?" her father asked.

She looked up startled. "No . . . . no, I guess not."

A call came in from one of her friends. "Can Kendra come with us to Disneyland?"

Do you want to go, sweetheart?" I didn't have space for my baby, even now, after all these weeks away.

"No . . . I want to stay with daddy."

"Well, he's going to sleep most of the time. I'm so tired, I want to sleep too. They can pick you up tonight to get an early start. They'll bring you home tomorrow. What do you say."

She shook her head. Then said, "Okay, I guess so, if that's what you want."

Harold and I lay on our bed, neither of us sleeping. We held on to the silence of our own room, our memories crowding out our grief. Over the next hour, Harold's breathing became more jagged. He shuddered. I heard a soft moan.

"Pain?" I held him gently. He didn't answer.

Finally he spoke. "The last place I want to be . . . ."

"What Harold?"

"The last place I want to be is in a hospital again. But I don't want any more stress for you. The end can get messy. Karlan, call George."

I drove slowly through the silent streets. Harold didn't want an ambulance.

"Sorry, my love." He touched my arm. "Sorry about all this. So much I want to tell you while I can."

I drove carefully not to jolt him. I didn't speak.

"Keep the house, okay?" He said it as if making a list for a weekend trip. "It's your best financial asset. You can do anything. Do you know that? You're so much stronger than I've ever been. I'm not worried about you in the long run—just the next few months."

"Harold, listen to me. Put this energy into hope. You're in the prime of your life." I looked over at him but his eyes were on the hospital just ahead.

George stood at the emergency door waiting for us. Harold got hooked up to machines again.

In the morning, Harold told me to buy Kendra a beautiful dress. "Please, it's important to me. And another thing, I want you to buy one just like it for . . . Is it Ann? I mean the girl she went to Disneyland with."

"Yes, that's her name but I don't want to, not now and we don't have any money."

"There's some in my wallet. Please, I want to give her a 'princess dress.'"

I went shopping. Harold slipped into a coma. He was transferred into I.C.U.

"He kept asking for you," the nurse told me. She shook her head bewildered by my absence. I didn't explain.

Our close friends gathered for the vigil. Kendra's return had been delayed because of car trouble. Rob wouldn't leave his father's side. Rick came and went. Finally, I told everyone to go home. I hugged both the boys. "I'll see you in the morning." They stared dry-eyed then backed out of the ICU cubical.

I sat alone for some hours listening to the sounds of a life fading away. The thought of so many others waiting, waiting just like me in the same chair—gave me solace. I didn't care about tomorrow, even the pain in the eyes of my sons didn't distract me. Harold was slipping away. I had no power, no magic to stop it. I didn't pray. I had been doing that for the last ten weeks. I felt utterly alone.

I knew. Ever cell in my body knew. I flew out of my chair to Harold's side just in time to see his last recorded heart beat. The drill to restart his life began. I put up my hand.

"Stop. He's gone. Give him peace."

# *Epilogue*

Kendra never wore her "princess dress." She felt betrayed. Her father had promised to walk her down the aisle at her wedding. He hadn't said anything about dying before her tenth birthday.

But I represented the greatest betrayal. I hadn't even let her tell her daddy goodbye.

Rick "lost" the last several months of his senior year in high school. He was in a daze of grief. The school understood and he graduated with his class. Without telling me, he enlisted in the air force to help pay our bills.

Rob buried his grief. He threw himself into study and sports.

Four years later, while attending a party with his buddies, he excused himself to use the restroom. His friends heard him scream, followed by sobbing.

"What's going on, Rob? What happened?" His friends pounded on the locked door.

What Rob answered came in a whisper. "My dad died."

The father of Rick's best friend took me under his wing. He taught me to budget and invested our meager life insurance money along with income from Harold's retirement fund. Jerry and others maneuvered to have debts forgiven. Eventually my investments flourished. I divided the house, rented to another family, worked in the elementary school system and took classes at night. Also I learned that my strange ailments were caused by systemic lupus erythematosus.

After a year, I began attending parties. Then, with great trepidation, graduated into dating. Doug stayed vital in my life. His letters continued to support me. We kept each other up-to-date about our social activities.

A year after Harold died, we learned my father had a malignant brain tumor. Joan and I got him out of the hospital and home so we could nurse him through his last days. Tenderness and understanding again became the energy between my father and me.

The day before he died, he began talking about our years in France. "I always felt sad that we didn't bring Mademoiselle Malmoray with us when we returned to America. You would still be speaking French."

I kept still. I didn't want my father to know anything about what had happened to me in the tool shed in Paris.

"Oh, well," he went on. "It's probably for the best. Just before we left, I learned that your nurse had some strange religious ideas."

My heart went cold.

Father stopped for a moment, closed his eyes trying to recall exactly what he had heard. "She's Catholic, of course, but she also kept faith with a more ancient religion. She believed witches were born by chance here and there. The trick to keeping the world safe, according to her religion, was not to let the innocent witches have babies."

My father must have thought my startled face and intake of breath meant only surprise that my nurse could believe such a thing.

"I heard," he continued, "she believed the Devil would only mate with a witch. Isn't that bizarre? Best she stayed in Paris."

Mother suffered a crushing stroke. She had not been expected to survive, certainly never walk again. The doctors didn't know my mother. She refused to stay in a wheelchair. Though her speech never returned, she could pantomime. I had little trouble understanding her. I wouldn't let her live with me because she was critical of Kendra. However I saw her often. We still struggled but we also learned to laugh together.

Two years after Harold died, mother made one of her frequent visits. At the same time, Doug planned to drop by on his way north. Mother and I were out front when he drove up in his vintage Volkswagen bus. When Doug climbed out, I caught my breath. Oh, how glad I was to see him. He looked handsome, warm, energetic. Mother stared. Her mouth hung open in surprise.

"Ri . . . s . . . fr . . . nd?" she struggled to ask.

"No mother, not Rick's friend, though he does look young enough. This is Doug. He's my friend. I've told you about him. Remember?"

After I introduced them, Doug carried a package of books into the house. Mother held my arm to keep me back. She gave me a look I couldn't figure out. Then in perfect clarity she said, "uu la la!" I smiled and nodded. But she had something else on her mind. She walked purposefully to the kitchen, opening cupboards.

"What are you looking for, mother?"

She shook her head as if to say, "Don't bother me." Triumphantly, she pulled out a box of tea.

"Would you like me to make you a cup?"

Again she shook her head, pulled out a bag, tore it open. The dry tea spilled into a cup on the counter. She watched me carefully.

"I don't understand. What do you want?"

Frustration filled her face. Next, she put water into the cup of tea leaves, tried to swirl it around. Water splattered everywhere. At last, I got it. A prickly heat rush of memory flooded me. I found myself back as a child listening to her prediction as she read my fortune in the leaves:

"Someday a tall, dark, handsome man with flashing eyes will love you. He'll make all your pain go away and fill your heart with joy."

The description fit Doug perfectly.

8146529R0

Made in the USA
Lexington, KY
14 January 2011